< HOW TO TALK ABOUT VIDEOGAMES >

Also by Ian Bogost
Published by the University of Minnesota Press

Alien Phenomenology, or What It's Like to Be a Thing

How to Do Things with Videogames

The Geek's Chihuahua: Living with Apple

HOW
TO
TALK
ABOUT
VIDEOGAMES

Ian Bogost

Electronic Mediations 47

University of Minnesota Press
Minneapolis
London

Earlier versions of chapters 1, 2, 7, 17, and 18 were previously published at *The Atlantic,* theatlantic.com. Earlier versions of chapters 3, 4, 8, 9, 10, 11, 12, 13, 15, and 19 were previously published at *Gamasutra,* gamasutra .com; reprinted with permission. An earlier version of chapter 6 was published as "Rage against the Machines: The Real Danger of Videogames Isn't Violence; It's Swindling," *Baffler* 24 (November 2013): 96–103; reprinted with permission. Portions of chapter 14 were previously published in Difficulty Switch column pieces in *Edge Magazine.* An earlier version of chapter 16 was published as "What Are Sports Videogames?" in *Sports Videogames,* edited by Mia Consalvo, Konstantin Mitgutsch, and Abe Stein (London: Routledge, 2014), 50–66. An earlier version of chapter 20 was published as "Perpetual Adolescence: The Fullbright Company's Gone Home," *Los Angeles Review of Books,* September 28, 2013; reprinted with permission.

Contents

Nobody Asked for a Toaster Critic

Doing game criticism

Imagine that your toaster has broken. Like any reasonable person, you want to replace it as quickly as possible so as to continue enjoying the delights of browned bread.

But there are so many options. Slot toaster or toaster oven? OK, that one's easy, toaster ovens are barbaric, but two-slot or four? Bagel-wide slot or a lithe, streamlined design? A chrome finish looks stylish, but you know that it will attract kitchen grease and quickly dull without constant care. An enameled, bright-hued finish might offer a pop of color, but you worry that a robin blue or canary yellow apparatus might soon wear out its welcome. So many options. Soon enough, the malaise of modern commerce overtakes you, the overwhelm that the psychologist Barry Schwartz has called the paradox of choice: as the number of possible options increases, the anguish of making a choice becomes more acute rather than less.[1]

What to do? Seek out information. You might turn to a friend or a family member whom you recall having fashioned particularly cracking toast on a recent visit. You could subscribe to *Consumer Reports* to find the model with the greatest number of that publication's characteristic red doughnuts of approval. More likely, you'd fire up Amazon.com and start browsing toasters. As I write, the number one seller is a ghastly ivory pod of a thing, the Hamilton Beach 2-Slice. Pass. A more stoic, Oster 4-slice catches your eye, its sturdy-looking knobs and handles flanking an attractive, grease-resistant brushed-chrome surface.

< vii >

Nearly four hundred reviews help clarify things further. A buyer from 2012 whose input is rated the "most helpful positive review" writes that the Oster is a "simple basic toaster that just works," awarding it five stars. At this point, you might call it a day and click "Buy Now," your angst giving way to the anticipation of fresh toast in only a day or two. Or you might continue browsing, in search of the model whose features, looks, reliability, and price match your tastes and tolerances.

What you probably wouldn't do is look for an essay on the *meaning* of the Oster 4-slice toaster. What would it mean for a toaster to mean something, anyway? A toaster doesn't exist to depict, to portray, to represent, to fashion dreams or nightmares. Nobody asked for a toaster critic. A toaster exists to caramelize bread. It's preposterous to think otherwise.

Unless it isn't.

Some of the possible meanings of toasters are obvious. A 4-slot toaster is a signal of throughput—the size of a family, the dryness of a palate. The chrome finish is a symbol of nostalgia; indeed, it seems most toasters are designed to recall a particular feeling of 1950s googie or 1930s streamline moderne design. These were moments when toast meant family and comfort (1950), and curved metal meant speed and progress (1930).

It's also why the toaster oven is so monstrous. On the one hand, it embraces the efficiencies of modern technological life, combining the necessity of bread browning with the convenience of a small, general-purpose oven. But on the other hand, it violates the concept of a toaster: a serious commitment to the caramelization of bread. To what other single-purpose appliance does the modern family devote a square foot of precious kitchen counter space? None. The toaster is not just an appliance: it is a life philosophy, one that knows that pleasure and opulence bubble out from the sugars in wheat risen to loaves. It turns out that toasters share something in common with televisions, with paintings, with furniture, with textiles—with all the other materials with which we surround ourselves and whose form and function establish and communicate our personal and social lives.

Videogames are a lot like toasters. We think they are appliances, mere tools that exist to entertain or distract. We think that their ability to satisfy our need for leisure is their only function. And as with electronics and consumer goods of all kinds, there are *Consumer Reports*–style videogame reviews, full of technical details and thorough testing and final, definitive scores delivered on improbably precise numerical scales. In the games industry, developer bonuses are even sometimes tied to the aggregated results of such reviews as measured by aggregators like Metacritic.[2]

But then, we also have to admit that games are something more than just nondescript vessels that deliver varying dosages of video pleasure. They include characters and personas with whom we can identify and empathize, like we might do with a novel or a film. They are composed of forms and designs derived from whole cloth, producing visual, tactile, and locomotive appeal like fashion or painting or furniture. They insert themselves into our lives, weaving within and between our daily practices, both structuring and disrupting them. They induce feelings and emotions in us, just as art or music or fiction might do. But then, games also extend well beyond the usual payloads of those other media, into frustration, anguish, physical exhaustion, and addictive desperation. Wagnerian Gesamtkunstwerk-flavored chewing gum.

When it comes to the role of criticism among toasters and videogames, confusion arises because both are *operated*: they do things, and the manner by which they do them matters. The result of their having been done matters. But the process and experience of that operation also matters. If videogames were just meant to inject the greatest enjoyment at the lowest cost per unit, they would just be inefficient, unintuitive narcotics.

Whether with toasters or videogames, the difference between the critic and the reviewer is that the critic recognizes both sides of his or her Janus-faced subject: the functional, operative one (the face that gets something done in the world) and the expressive, formal one (the face that puts that operation in context and makes the operation of the device more than just a machine spewing output onto a counter or a television display).

Unlike the reviewer, the critic of functional gizmos like games and toasters decouples himself or herself from the proverbial toast that the object of criticism fashions. If the reviewer speaks from a position of investment, the critic speaks from a position of remove. Not just remove from the work, but also at a remove from oneself. Unlike the artist or the designer or even the writer, the critic's work is oriented not around the self but around the other.

This means that being a critic is not an enjoyable job. I mean that in the most practical, ordinary sense of the word: criticism is not pleasurable. It's not as bad as being a coal miner or an actuary, although at least miners and actuaries get paid for their efforts. But just as it is hard to do criticism for pay, so it is harder to do for gratification. The critic speaks in his or her own voice not primarily to give voice to that voice but to speak through it, to catalog and to clarify the world.

Good criticism tends to do this by answering the question "What is even going on here?" This is the question that audiences don't even know they want answered. They don't know what to ask. They are awash in a barrage of noise that only the critic can tune into signal. What is my kid doing all the time in *Minecraft*? Why can't I stop playing *Flappy Bird* even though I hate it? Do I even hate it, or is this sensation I am naming "hate" something else entirely? Why is everyone talking about *Titanfall*? And later, why did they suddenly stop talking about it?

Unlike the artist, the critic makes no appeal to something that "had to come out." The critic answers questions, starting with the most fundamental question: what *is* this thing? Why does it exist? And then the critic answers questions that offer relief: What do I do with it? What am I not seeing that I don't know I'm missing? What will cure the sickness that I don't even know I have?

You can see it in toasters as much as in videogames. A 2013

review of our unlikely hero, the Oster 4-slice, offers only two stars beside the melancholy title "What happened to toasters?" Sure, some *Consumer Reports*–type analysis comes along for the ride. The toaster's outside surface becomes unreasonably hot, according to this critic. He theorizes that poor insulation leads to unexpected heat transfer (he doesn't use these words) yielding inconsistent results. But it's that opening question—*what happened to toasters?*—that carries the day. "I am living with this one for now," the critic writes, "and trying to master its idiosyncrasies." It's the ultimate truth about toast, isn't it? Somehow, somewhere inside that magic box, bread becomes toast. Seemingly so simple, yet even in mere caramelization the universe admits enough entropy to produce chaos. (Technically, the delight of toast is caused by the *Maillard reaction,* named for the early twentieth-century French chemist who described the interaction between amino acids and sugars in browned foods like toast, seared steak, roasted coffee, and fried potatoes.)

This is just an Amazon review, of course, and it doesn't match the existential angst and absurdity one finds in the most creative critiques hosted by our amiable online retailer overlord—those for Uranium Ore, for example, or the more than fifteen hundred legendary reviews for Tuscan Whole Milk, 1 Gallon, 128 fl oz.[3] The latter includes everything from rhyming couplets to meta-commentary on the product review process itself to pop culture reference to performative wordplay that reframes this ordinary commodity as a luxury potation. This last variety is my favorite, perhaps: "I find Venetian whole milk far superior," it begins, before ruminating, "Provençal is even better. It has hints of lavender. But it's a rare vintage."

And with a toaster or a gallon of mail-order milk, there is something preposterous about writing criticism—particularly criticism of objects we use as much as experience. This is probably why whenever I write criticism of videogames, someone strongly invested in games as a hobby always asks the question "is this parody?" as if only a miscreant or a comedian or a psychopath would bother to invest the time and deliberateness in even *thinking,* let alone writing about videogames with the seriousness that random, anonymous Internet users have already used to write about toasters, let alone deliberate intellectuals about film or literature! It's an annoying, dumbfounding question, of course, an insult that betrays the very same individual's likely demand that games be treated as seriously as other cultural forms, "as art," even, to use a cliché that's gone stale.

Like a toaster, a game is both appliance and hearth, both instrument and aesthetic, both gadget and fetish. It's preposterous to do game criticism, like it's preposterous to do toaster criticism. But that preposterousness also points to why and how criticism exists. Criticism is not conducted to improve the work or the medium, or to win over those who otherwise would turn up their noses at it. Nor is it conducted as flash-in-the-pan buying advice, doled out on release day to reverie or disdain, only to be immediately forgotten. Rather, it is conducted to get to the bottom of something, to grasp its form, context, function, meaning, and capacities. To venture so far from the ordinariness of a subject that the terrain underfoot gives way from manicured path to wilderness, so far that the words that we would spin tousle the hair of madness. And then, to preserve that wilderness and its madness, such that both the works and our reflections on them become imbricated with one another and carried forward into the future where others might find them anew.

Really, nothing was ever immune to the preposterousness of committed attention that criticism entails. Not literature, not film, nor theater, art, food, wine. We just stopped noticing that the criticism of forms like these are just as bonkers as critiques of toasters or milk or videogames. Just as bonkers only because we unwittingly collapsed the functional and expressive sides of an HBO show or a Spanish Tempranillo into the silly, false dream of mere artfulness. That lost memory is no worse than treating games just as gadgets to be reviewed instrumentally, as commodities rated on scales of ten—and no worse than treating them as just expressions of poignant emotion, either.

How to talk about videogames? Like a critic, not a reviewer, for one, but also: like a toaster critic, not just a film critic. To do game criticism is to take this common-born subject as toaster and as savior, as milk and as wine, as idiocy and as culture.

This is a book full of such specimens—attempts to take games so seriously as to risk the descent into self-parody. Or even, to embrace that descent, since caricature is another means to truth. For there, far, far away from ordinary life and ordinary pleasure, familiar devices become unfamiliar, such that we can appreciate them for what they are rather than what we wish them to be.

1

The Squalid Grace of *Flappy Bird*

Why playing stupid games staves off existential despair

Games are grotesque.

I'm not talking about games like *Grand Theft Auto* or *Manhunt,* games whose subjects are moral turpitude, games that ask players to murder, maim, destroy. I mean games in general, the form we call "games." Games are gross, revolting heaps of arbitrary anguish. Games are encounters with squalor. You don't play a game to experience an idea so much as you do so in an attempt to get a broken machine to work again.

In this way, games are different from other media. Sure, a movie or a book or a painting can depict squalor, can attune us to the agony of misfortune. But unlike film and literature, games do not primarily depict human events and tell stories. And unlike sports, games do not primarily showcase physical prowess. We don't watch or read games like we do cinema and novels and paintings, nor do we perform them like we might dance or football or Frisbee. Rather, we do something in-between with games. Yes, we "play" games like we do sports, and yes, games bear "meaning," as do the fine and plastic arts. But something else is at work in games. Games are devices we operate.

Sometimes that operation simulates piloting a mecha or a pro athlete or a space marine, but more frequently it entails more mundane activities: moving cards between stacks as in Klondike solitaire; swapping adjacent gems as in *Bejeweled*; directing a circular, discarnate maw as in *Pac-Man*. Some machinery is fantastic, but most is ordinary, forgettable, broken.

< 1 >

If you look past the familiar shimmer of *Super Mario Bros.* and Super Bowl Sunday, there in the middle you will find the unsung paragons of gaming: games like chess and backgammon; tic-tac-toe and dots and boxes and crosswords; Monopoly and Candy Land and Sorry! These are games that frustrate more than they titillate, because operating them involves minimal effort yet considerable misery. It's not the misery of boredom or stupidity but the misery of repetition. The misery of knowing what you want to accomplish but not being able to, whether thanks to the plodding pace of a child's board game or the bottomless strategic depth of a folk classic. Whereas football yields its beauty through the practiced triumph of the human body and will over circumstance, Sorry! delivers only the stupid, gratuitous anguish caused by our decision to play it in the first place.

Every now and then a game comes along that forces us to admit this inconvenient truth of games. The feral Apple App Store once was graced with such a one, a free mobile throwaway called *Flappy Bird.* The game was first released in the summer of 2013, but as that year wound down, it experienced an unexpected surge in popularity. By the start of 2014, the title had nested itself at the top of the App Store's free charts.

Flappy Bird is a stupid game. You control a bird so cute as to signal deformity. Tapping the screen causes the bird to flap, making it rise slightly before quickly falling. The game asks only that you pilot the bird through narrow passageways between two green, Super Mario–style pipes that issue from the top and bottom of the screen. A point is awarded for every pipe you pass. But touch anything, and the cute bird tumbles beak-first into the ground: game over.

Flappy Bird is a perversely, oppressively difficult game. Scoring even a single point takes most players a considerable number of runs. After an hour, I'd managed a high score of two. Many, many hours of play later, my high score was thirty-two, a feat that earned me the game's gold medal (whatever that means).

There is a tradition of such super-difficult games, sometimes called *masocore* among the videogame savvy. Masocore games are normally characterized by trial-and-error gameplay, but split up into levels or areas to create a sense of overall progress. Commercial blockbusters like *Mega Man* inaugurated the category (even if the term *masocore* appeared long after Capcom first released that title in 1987), and more recent independent titles like *I Wanna Be the Guy* and *Super Meat Boy* have further explored the idea of intense difficulty as a primary aesthetic. Combined with repetition and progression, the intense difficulty of masocore games often produces a feeling of profound accomplishment, an underdog's victory in the dorky medium of underdogs themselves, 2-D platformer videogames.

Even though *Flappy Bird* borrows from the same platformer tradition, it's no masocore game. For one part, masocore is more of an aesthetic community than it is a material aesthetic; like the poetry and painting that emerged from the Pre-Raphaelite Brotherhood, masocore games arise from a dedication to a particular kind of play experience, or perhaps even more so a disgust with the rise of facile, "everybody wins" casual games since the turn of the millennium.

But *Flappy Bird* is not difficult because it wants to oppose any regime in particular, a fact made flesh by its deployment on the mobile platforms that have only accelerated casual play. *Flappy Bird* is not difficult to challenge you, or even to teach the institution of videogames a thing or two. Rather, *Flappy Bird* is difficult because it is indifferent, like an iron gate rusted shut, like the unexpected ice storm that shuts down a city. It's not hard for the sake of your experience; it's just hard because that's the way it is. Where masocore games want nothing more than to please their players with pain and humiliation (thus their appropriation of the term *masochism*), *Flappy Bird* just exists. It wants nothing and expects even less.

The game seems to have come from out of nowhere. It was created by a lone, twenty-nine-year-old Vietnamese developer named Dong Nguyen, who mostly denied requests for press interviews after his game's explosive success. Nguyen had previously released several other games with a similar avant-pixel aesthetic and simple gameplay. While tech press outlets accustomed to megalomaniac entrepreneurs motivated only by fame and wealth reframed the creator's timidity as "mystery,"[1] Nguyen's own words likely explain the situation more accurately: "The popularity could be my luck."[2]

Nguyen's status as outsider artist may be the key to the game's deftly indifferent design, even if it can't explain its success. Nguyen's earlier games were much rougher and less refined than *Flappy Bird*. In *Shuriken Block,* the player taps on the screen to deflect throwing stars that would otherwise lodge in the heads of a row of cute pixel samurai. A correct tap issued more quickly yields more points than one at the last minute. But an observant player can simply turn the game into a joke, tapping constantly at the top of the screen to achieve as high a score as patience affords. In *Super Ball Juggling,* the player taps the right and left sides of the screen to individually control two soccer players juggling balls that rise to different heights with each bounce. After a few singular practice juggles, balls appear simultaneously on both sides, and the player must struggle against the absence of a continuous rhythm to perform well at the game.

But rather than improve on these and other game design techniques, *Flappy Bird* actually regresses, offering fewer rather than more crutches for either novice or expert play. It even withdraws from the gentler onboarding of *Super Ball Juggling.* Contemporary design practice surely would recommend an "easy" first pipe sequence to get the player started, perhaps a few pipes positioned at the bird's initial position, or with wider openings for easier passage. More difficult maneuvers, such as quick shifts from high to low pipe openings, would be reserved for later in the game, with difficulty ramping up as the player demonstrates increased expertise.

But *Flappy Bird* offers no such scaffolding. Instead, every pipe and every point is utterly uniform: randomly positioned but indistinguishable in every other way. A game of *Flappy Bird* is a series of identical maneuvers, one after the other. All you have to do is keep responding to them, a task made possible by the game's predictable and utterly reasonable interactions. Just keep flapping.

This indifference to player capacity and expectation makes *Flappy Bird* a particularly earnest device to operate. Many players expressed astonishment and distress at their simultaneous hatred for and commitment to the game—"I Hate Flappy Bird, But I Can't Stop Playing It"—essentially concluding that the game is just another "addictive" trifle, a curiosity that cannot be understood despite spilling ink in the effort.[3] Meanwhile, the tech press continues its tendency to present business *as* aesthetics, limiting its coverage of *Flappy Bird* to the game's viral success (millions of daily downloads).[4] It also explains the gold rush insurgence of copycat games like *Ironpants,* which mistake *Flappy Bird's* surprise success for a predictable design pattern rather than a confluence of accidents.

In game design circles, we sometimes wax poetic about the elegance and simplicity of a design, the way complex emergent behaviors can arise from simple rules and structures. This is why game designers tend to love games like Go and *Tetris*—tiny flowers that betray their simplicity by divulging endless fractal blossoms.

But in fetishizing simplicity, we also mistake the elegance of design for beauty. For Go and *Tetris* are likewise ghastly, erupting stones and tetrominoes endlessly, failing to relent in their desire to overtake us. The games we find ourselves ever more devoted to are often also the ones that care little for our experience of them. This is the devotion of material indifference. To understand *Flappy Bird,* we must accept the premise that games are squalid, rusty machinery we operate despite themselves. What we appreciate about *Flappy Bird* is not the details of its design but the fact that it embodies them with such unflappable nonchalance. The best games cease to be for us (or for anyone) and instead strive to be what they are as much as possible. From this indifference emanates a strange squalor that we can appreciate as beauty.

Let me explain what I mean by way of analogy. The day before I fell prey to the *Flappy Bird* phenomenon, I spent two hours attempting to fix a bathroom cabinet drawer pull that comes unattached on one side, hanging despondently at the bottom of the vanity. I detached the hardware and confirmed that the handle happily accepted the machine screw into its threads, but somehow the two weren't meshing when set in the drawer front. I drilled to widen the hole through which the screw passed, noting that the screw seemed to require a precise orthogonal orientation to thread properly. I swapped both orientations and screws, thinking that I'd achieve a more accurate alignment. I deployed penlights and vice grips. My family began receding ever farther into the house, aware of the dark shadow that grew from the bathroom, where an oiled bronze drawer pull siphoned vitality from our residence and, perhaps, from the universe itself.

A commitment to *Flappy Bird* is akin to the sensation after two hours splayed on the floor of your bathroom, when you still haven't managed to reattach the cabinet pull that somehow won't stay attached to the drawer, even though the hardware happily accepts the machine screw when you hold both pieces in your hand. Emergence is also chaos, and its charm is the beauty of a universe that could have been nothing, but turned out to be something instead. That something is both revolting and divine, and we cheat ourselves when we take the one alone without the other.

Compared with other games, *Flappy Bird* offers a more ardent take on unconcern. Instead of relying on the exploding permutational space of a few, easily memorizable gestures, it relies on the cold fury of sheer repetition instead. Like Candy Land, that scourge of preschools and pediatrician offices, *Flappy Bird* demands only that you do the same thing again and again, until something else interrupts you—and then it removes the only guarantee of interruption Candy Land affords, that of a certain victory and an excuse to put the game away.

And not for lack of other options, either. *Flappy Bird* is hardly a new design—it follows in the footsteps of a genre now known as the "endless runner," named after the 2009 mobile hit *Canabalt,* in which players help a man outrun an unseen threat that destroys the city whose rooftops he traverses to escape. *Canabalt* begat similar titles, including the massive hit *Temple Run,* whose sequel was installed over fifty million times in two weeks.

The endless runner itself has a lineage, which *Flappy Bird* likewise spurns. Writing in the *New Yorker,* Simon Parkin traced the origins of the genre first to a frequently re-created DOS game with a helicopter in an endless tunnel, and before that to a 1983 Commodore 64 game, *B.C.'s Quest for Tires,* based on the classic caveman comic strip by Johnny Hart.[5] But even three decades ago, *B.C.'s Quest for Tires* offers more sophistication than *Flappy Bird.* The caveman on his stone unicycle must avoid multiple obstacles—jumping rocks, ducking under trees, avoiding rolling stones, and so forth—while enduring regular increases in the speed of progress.

Set in relief against its precursors, *Flappy Bird* seems positively minimalist. The Zen garden school of design would encourage us to interpret this choice as more rather than less sophisticated: by removing all unnecessary elements, the purity of the endless runner is revealed. This sounds good on paper, but the experience of *Flappy Bird* betrays it. "Surely something else will happen?" asks the *Flappy Bird* player, over and over. But nothing ever does. This isn't a surplus of design thanks to unadornment but a brazen opposition to modernist elegance through the austere design that tradition holds so dear. This discomfort echoes all throughout the *Flappy Bird* experience. Is it just a *bad* minimalist runner, or is it purposely disparaging the genre it adopts?

The answer is neither: *Flappy Bird* is not amateurish or sociopathic. Instead, it is something more unusual. It is earnest. It is exactly what it is, and it is unapologetic. Not even unapologetic—stoic, aloof. Impervious. Like a meteorite that crashed through a desert motel lobby, hot and small and unaware.

Playing *Flappy Bird* is like fixing an unfixable drawer pull, one that will never reattach correctly, one that you *know* will never do, but persisting in the face of such torpor nevertheless. *Flappy Bird* is a condition of the universe, even if it is one that didn't exist until it was hand-crafted by a Vietnamese man who doesn't want to talk about it. A *condition* in the sense of a circumstance, but also in the sense of a blight, a sickness, a stain we cannot scrub out but may in time be willing to accept. A stain like our own miserable, tiny existences as players, which we nevertheless believe are more fundamental than the existence of bird-flapping games or machine screws or the cold fog rising against the melting snow in the morning. Because the game cares so little for your experience of it, you find yourself ever more devoted to it.

Mere moments after its explosive rise, Dong Nguyen dramatically pulled *Flappy Bird* from the Apple App Store and Google Play, claiming it was too addictive. "I just wanted to create a game that people could enjoy for a few minutes," he told the *Wall Street Journal*. On the one hand, one can't help but admire Nguyen for apparently sacrificing the enormous sums *Flappy Bird* had been earning from advertising (up to $50,000 per day, according to some reports), especially at a time when the biggest mobile and social games companies will do anything to make a buck. But Nguyen's apparent sacrifice quickly degrades into its own opportunism. For just as *Flappy Bird*'s design issues forth an intransigent apathy for its players, so the game's surprising and improbable success circulates a similar unconcern for its creator. After all, why should Nguyen derive uncomplicated satisfaction from his creation any more than his players should do from its operation? Nguyen's error was not in making *Flappy Bird* but in failing to see it from a creator's perspective as the challenge against reason, decorum, and comfort it so ably issued to its players.

We like to think of games as an entertainment medium on the move. As a contender to replace (or at least to match) the influence and appeal of literature, film, painting, dance, sculpture. As a way to present ideas and experiences through our most contemporary of vessels, the computer. We may often play games because they affect us, because they allow us to be someone fantastic and unassailable. But games are also ancient, and ancient things teach us humility. Just as often, we play games because they are there to be played. Because we want to feel what it's like to play them. Because we are not clever or strong or fast, but because we can move stones on wooden boards or shift cards between virtual spaces on cardboard or tap a capacitive display to flap a tiny bird.

We play games because games are stupid, like drawer pulls are stupid. *Flappy Bird* is a game that accepts that it is stupid to be a game. It offers us an example of what it might feel like to conclude that this is enough. That it's enough for games just to be crap in the universe, detritus that we encounter from time to time and that we might encounter *as* detritus rather than as meaning. That we might stop to manipulate them without motive or reason, like we might turn a smooth rock in our palms before tossing it back into the big ocean, which devours it. For no matter how stupid it is to be a game, it is no less stupid to be a person who plays one.

2

A Portrait of the Artist as a Game Studio

The aesthetic trajectory of thatgamecompany's *flOw,*
Flower, and *Journey*

Artists' aesthetics evolve and deepen over time. You can see it in
their work, as immaturity and coarseness give way to sophistication and polish. In most media, an audience witnesses this aesthetic evolution take place within the most mature form of that
medium, the materials professionals and amateurs alike share.

Between the 1930s and the 1950s, for example, the abstract
expressionist painter Mark Rothko's work evolved from mythical surrealism to multiform abstractions to his signature style of
rectilinear forms. Different motivations and inspirations moved
Rothko during these two decades, but at every stage of his artistic career, the painter's work could be experienced as painting, as
medium on canvas. As flatness and pigment on linen.

Likewise, the contemporary American novelist Ben Marcus
has explored his unique brand of experimental fiction in three
novels, and his style and effect have changed and deepened as
his writing career has progressed. Marcus's 1995 novel *The Age*
of Wire and String uses a technical perversion of English that
the author coerces into fantastic and nearly inscrutable tales of
rural life. The 2002 follow-up *Notable American Women* refines
his semantic surrealism into a more legible narrative, but one
in which language itself remains untrustworthy. And in 2012's
Flame Alphabet, Marcus reaches a new summit, a book in which

< 10 >

language kills from the inside out. Once more, an artist births and refines experimental style, but carries out that evolution within the standard form of the art in question: the offset-printed hardback book.

Aesthetic evolution need not move from lesser to greater effect. Since 1999 M. Night Shyamalan has practiced his signature brand of filmmaking, in which supernatural situations end in dramatic plot twists. But between *The Sixth Sense* (1999) and *The Last Airbender* (2010), Shyamalan's artistic success faltered even as his films continued to perform well at the box office. Decline notwithstanding, still, all his films were printed to celluloid and projected onto anamorphic wide-screen cinema screens.

In painting, literature, and film the public can see an artist's work evolve (or devolve) because that work is accessible to audiences in their native forms. Archivists or scholars might dig into a creator's sketchbooks or retrieve early works, but such museum work is not required for the ordinary viewer or reader to grasp the changes and refinements of work over time. This perception of creative progress is a part of the pleasure of art, whether through the joy of growth or the schadenfreude of decay.

In videogames, it's far less common to see a creator's work evolve in this way. In part, this is because game makers tend to have less longevity than other sorts of artists. In part, it's because games are more highly industrialized even than film, and aesthetic headway is often curtailed by commercial necessity. And in part, it's because games are so tightly coupled to consumer electronics that technical progress outstrips aesthetic progress in the public imagination.

Where there are game makers with a style, it has often evolved over long durations. Will Wright's discovery and later mastery of the software toy simulation, from *SimCity* to *SimEarth* to *The Sims*; or John Carmack and John Romero's revolutionary exploitation of new powers in real-time 2-D and 3-D graphics in *Commander Keen, Doom,* and *Quake*; or Hideo Kojima's development and refinement of the stealth action games of the *Metal*

Gear series, characterized by solitude, initial weakness, cinematic cut-scenes, and self-referential commentary.

These styles evolved over decades, and they did so in the arms of financial success and corporate underwriting. Structurally speaking, they are more like Shyamalan than like Rothko and Marcus, the latter two artists having struggled to find their respective styles outside the certainty of commercial success.

In independent games, wherein we must hope that aesthetics ought to drive creators more than commercialism, creative evolution often takes place in tentative ways, in forms far less refined and mature than the videogame console that serves as the medium's equivalent to the cinema or the first-run hardback. Experimental titles may take their first form on a PC or a mobile device as humble experiments. If very fortunate, as have been game makers like Jonathan Blow (*Braid*), Jonathan Mak (*Everyday Shooter*), or Kyle Gabler and Ron Carmel (*World of Goo*), those games might find their way to the Nintendo or the Xbox or the PlayStation. But today, the artists who work in game development for its beauty before its profitability typically don't get to choose the most public of venues in which to experiment and come of age artistically.

Thatgamecompany's title *Journey* was an exception. The game is the third in a three-deal exclusive that the studio's principals signed with Sony right out of grad school at the University of Southern California. Thanks to the Sony exclusive and the oversight of Sony's Santa Monica studio, all three games targeted the PlayStation 3 from the beginning. This is not a remarkable feat for a Rothko or a Marcus—such artists simply pick up the generic media of canvas or page and work with them directly. But the PS3 was tightly controlled, and its development kits were expensive. The machine sets a high bar, too—a complex multicore architecture with streamlined coprocessors meant to enhance speed and throughput for specialized tasks, especially vector processing for graphical rendering.

Thatgamecompany's work thus offers us an unusual window

into the creative evolution of a game maker, one in which the transition from students to venerable artists took place before our very eyes over a short half-decade on a single and very public videogame platform.

During graduate school, thatgamecompany's creative director, Jenova Chen, became obsessed with the psychologist Mihaly Csikszentmihalyi's concept of flow, the psychological feeling of being fully involved in an experience. Csikszentmihalyi's book on the subject was published in 1990, but a definition for the phenomenon is often cribbed from a 1996 *Wired* interview: "Being completely involved in an activity for its own sake. The ego falls away. Time flies. Every action, movement, and thought follows inevitably from the previous one, like playing jazz. Your whole being is involved, and you're using your skills to the utmost."[1] In musical terms, flow means being *in the groove*; in athletic terms, we call it being *in the zone*. Flow is a state of being, one in which a task's difficulty is perfectly balanced against a performer's skill, resulting in a feeling of intense, focused attention.

Chen devoted his MFA thesis to the application of flow in games.[2] In his interpretation, flow can be graphed on a two-dimensional axis, challenge on the horizontal axis and ability on the vertical. He then identifies a space surrounding the line that extends from low challenge and ability to high, which he calls the "flow zone." This zone is nestled between anxiety above (too much challenge, insufficient ability) and boredom below (not enough challenge, too much ability). Different players, argues Chen, have different flow zones, representing higher and lower capacities for each.

Chen contends that to reach broader audiences, games need to fit a wider variety of flow zones, either by expanding those zones or by adjusting the game to better match a specific player's zone. The latter could be done implicitly through automated adjustment or explicitly through player choice.

To illustrate this principle, Chen and several USC colleagues made a slick, abstract online game aptly titled *flOw*. In the game, the player controls a microorganism in a pool of water. Eating loose bits (or the bits of other, smaller creatures) grows the player's creature. Two types of orbs allow the player to dive deeper into the murk, where the enemies are slightly more threatening, or to rise to a level above.

It was *flOw* that led Sony to sign Chen and his collaborators, including USC students Kellee Santiago, Nick Clark, and John Edwards. The PS3 version, released in 2007, is really just a fancier and more beautiful version of the Flash original.

You can see what Chen was aiming for: *flOw* was meant to allow players to move through the game at their own pace, either adjusting challenge by diving deeper or by adjusting ability by devouring more creature bits. But there was a problem.

Even though the game ticked the boxes Chen had theorized, the player controls the creatures by manipulating the pitch and yaw axes of the gyroscopic sixaxis controller. This awkward interface can't be tuned by player or by machine. The strange and surprising exertion that the game demands is further amplified by its mildly hallucinogenic, throbbing visuals. Chen's theory of flow in games hadn't taken account of the interface and environmental elements, but only the game's system.

Another factor contributed to a dissonance between *flOw* in practice and flow in theory. In creating his model of flow zones in games, Chen simplified Csikszentmihalyi's approach significantly. For Csikszentmihalyi, flow does not exist between anxiety and boredom; those states correspond with high challenge/low skill and low challenge/medium skill, respectively. True flow does not exist all along the line bisecting the two axes, but only at its top-rightmost corner, where *both* challenge and skill are highest.

The combination of these two factors reveal the game's flaw: being *in the zone* or *in the groove* may seem like a type of hallucinatory, out-of-body experience, but it's really a practice of awareness so deep that it moves beyond conscious decision. *flOw* externalized the quietude and smoothness of flow into the game's visual aesthetics, which are truly striking. But the experience itself suggests a misinterpretation rather than an embrace of Csikszentmihalyi. Flow is a matter not of planning and comfort but of deep, durable expertise.

Thatgamecompany's 2008 follow-up, *Flower,* could be called a three-dimensional, representational version of *flOw.* Instead of a multicellular creature, the player controls the wind, blowing flower petals through the air with the pitch and roll axes of the sixaxis controller. By flying near other flowers, the player's wind gust can pick up additional petals, and the groups of petals can be used to unlock or "enliven" dead zones—restoring life and color in a world dark with industry.

If *flOw* erred on the side of behavior, *Flower* steered too far in the direction of environment. The game is so lush and beautiful, with its wafting grasses and rosy sunsets, that the repetitive petal-collecting experience detracts from an otherwise idyllic experience of visitation. Where *flOw* proved violent and delirious, *Flower* became overdemanding and distracting, a nuisance of a game getting in the way of the experience of its gorgeous computer scenery.

Like Goldilocks's porridge, *Journey* reconciles these two poles: neither too anxious nor too distracting, the game finally admits that the application of flow in games is best left to those that allow mastery at the highest levels of skill and challenge—games like basketball and *Street Fighter* and chess and Go and *Starcraft*. *Journey* foregoes abstract, dynamically adjusted gameplay in favor of simple exploration, which allows the player to enjoy the haunting desert civilization the game erects from invented, abstract myth.

As it turns out, the appealing aspects of *flOw* and *Flower* would be found less in their openness to new players through tunable gameplay and more in the unique and striking worlds they created for players to explore.

The modest environment of *flOw* was already enough; the turquoise, shallow murk giving way to threatening dark blue as the player descends into the ocean that is the game's setting. The undiscovered creatures darken the shadows below, previewing them in a deft visual portent. The game's relative difficulty or facility never had anything on the tiny intrigue of a droplet. For its part, *Flower* offered a world rather than a microcosm, but it forced the player to focus on its fauna, and eventually the tenuous couplings between the human-made world and the natural one. These settings were the stars of the games.

Journey finally learns this lesson. Set in a mysterious, mythical desert civilization, the game abandons the cloying framing of *Flower*'s levels, which claimed to offer the dreams of citybound buds. Instead, *Journey* explains nothing and apologizes for nothing. Like *Star Wars* or *Spirited Away*, *Journey* makes the correct assumption that a bewitching, lived-in world is enough.

So much goes unanswered in *Journey*, from the very first screen. The creatures are humanoid but not human, or not identifiably so. They have eyes and dark skin, or else eyes but no faces. The desert dunes are littered with monuments—are they path markers? Tombstones? Relics? Advertisements? Sandfalls douse chasms lined with temples dressed in patterns reminiscent of Islamic geometric art. Fabric banners flap in the breeze awaiting the player's touch. Pixel shaders push synesthesia: the yellow sands feel hot somehow, and the pink sands cool. One environment—"level" seems too prosaic a word here—is cast entirely in shadow, and the blue sand and rising ribbons pay homage to the underwater worlds of *flOw*.

In *Journey*, thatgamecompany finally discovered that facility was never the design problem it was looking for. Its games are about the feeling of *being somewhere*, not about the feeling of solving something.

Thatgamecompany's titles are elemental, each pursuing a precise characterization of a material form. For *flOw*, it was water. For *Cloud* (another student game that predates the studio), vapor. For *Flower*, grass. And for *Journey*, sand. In *flOw*, these materials surround the player. In *Cloud*, the player ejects them. In *Flower*, the player passes through them on the way elsewhere. But in *Journey*, the sand has texture: it slips under the player's nomad at times, its dunes force it back at others. It covers the air like murk, and when pushed to its limits flips into snow.

These materials and environments make *Journey*, partly for their conception and partly thanks to the smooth, delightful rendering that John Edwards and his engineers manage to squeeze out of the PS3. The machine may have implicitly promised enormous, realistic game environments like those of *Red Dead Redemption* or *Saints Row*, but *Journey* shows that the world is fashioned from its tiny details as much as its cities.

Journey also—finally—abandons the sixaxis control in favor of the more conventional analog stick convention (although the device can be tilted to look in different directions). While I suspect that the designers feared that they might descend into the ghetto of the adventure game by making such a compromise, instead the more traditional controls allow the serenity and mystery that has been on the surface of each of their previous games to embrace the reality of experience and not just the theory of design.

Indeed, given the usual subjects of videogames, players would be forgiven to mistake *Journey*'s title for an adventure. The hero's journey is a common theme in videogames, but that formula requires a call to adventure, an ordeal, a reward, and a return. *Journey* offers none of these features, but something far more modest instead.

When the game starts, the player ascends a sand dune to a view of a tall mountain with a slit peak. The destination is implied, but no reason given. To progress, the player crosses the sands to discover and collect orbs that extend a scarf on his or her robes. When filled with the symbols imbued by orbs or cloth, the player can fly briefly to reach new summits or avoid obstacles. The same symbols line the walls of the game's temple ruins and emanate above the player to signal others and carry out actions—a lost language with no meaning implied or deciphered.

As the player moves from dunes to temples to lost cities, she must spread energy to neglected apparatuses. Just as the player's scarf lightens her feet, so cloth seems generally transformative in *Journey*'s universe. These cloth portals spread bridges over chasms at times and unleash fabric birds and jellyfish at others.

Fantastic, yes, but not a hero's journey. Insofar as it has one, it seems impossible not to read the game's story allegorically instead of mythically: an individual progresses from weakness, or birth, or ignorance, or an origin of any kind, through discovery and challenge and danger and confusion, through to completion. It could be a coming of age, or a metaphor for life, or an allegory of love or friendship or work or overcoming sickness or sloughing off madness. It could mean anything at all.

Thatgamecompany should be both praised and faulted for taking such a morally, culturally, and religiously ambiguous position; surely every sect and creed will be able to read its favorite meaning onto the game. On the one hand, this move underscores thatgamecompany's sophistication: in a medium where interpretation is scorned as indulgent and pretentious, *Journey* gives no ground: the player must bring something to the table.

On the other hand, the careful player may find the result as barren as it is receptive. After each environment, a white figure (a god? a mother? the mind's mirror? the artist's muse?) incants silently to the player's red-robed humanoid. When she does, recent events are added to an inscription of the journey thus far, rendered as if in symbol on rock or papyrus. But not just *thus far,* also a bit farther, the theme of the next scene revealed in abstract, hieroglyphic form. Is the future being foretold, or is everyone's future always the same? In a very real way, the latter is true for *Journey,* as everyone's journey through the game follows the same overall progression through the same environments. With one exception.

That *Journey* is an online game is a mystery many players may never discover. The game itself never makes any such claims, and as a downloadable (the format of its original release) it arrives with no manual or instructions. Save for a subtle nod at the end of the game's credits (which many players may overlook or miss entirely), only reviews and interviews with the creators reveal a feature whose extensive design and engineering become the silent center of the game, the wind that moves it.

Sometimes while you play, the game will invisibly match you up with another PlayStation owner who is also playing in the same environment. There's not much you can do with your companion—speech isn't possible, but touching each other refills the energy in the cloth of both characters' scarves. Pressing one of the controller buttons emits a ping that can help a player find his companion and, when used improvisationally, might allow basic signaling. Only one companion appears at a time, although a player might encounter many over the course of the game.

These encounters with the other are both touching and disturbing. For one part, there is no mistaking a companion for an artificial intelligence; it moves too erratically, or speeds ahead to steal the next objective too definitively, or falls behind too listlessly. Even given the minimal actions of *Journey,* somehow these ghost players appear rounder than most of the scripted, voice-acted characters in contemporary videogames.

For another part, you don't really play *with* these other players. They are there with you, doing what you do, helping at times and hindering at others, plodding senselessly toward a mountain peak that has no meaning save for that imbued by a few foreboding, pregnant camera pans. You're comforted by their presence. It's like sitting on the couch close to someone, watching TV.

Journey's anonymous multiplayer interactions are touching, but they are also tragic, like a Samuel Beckett novel with characters in red robes mumbling "I can't go on, I'll go on" in inscrutable pictograms. At one point in the deep scarlet shadow of the caves, I swear I saw my companion crumble to dust. If only Jean-Paul Sartre had known that one could always just turn off the console, *Matrix*-style.

If *Journey*'s journey is anyone's, then it can mean anything we make of it. But a tabula rasa carries all meaning and no meaning all at once. For me, the journey was less my own than that of thatgamecompany itself, a band of students stumbling toward improbable success and surfing it clumsily at first, but then more certainly.

At the time of *Journey*'s release, thatgamecompany's crew was still largely made up of USC Interactive Media Division MFA alumni, a division of the institution's famed cinema school. It's no wonder that their games are cinematic, not only in appearance and duration (*Journey* lasts a little over two hours), but also in structure. *Journey* and *Flower* demonstrate a rare mastery of the *denouement* in games. Good filmic storytellers end their tales quickly and definitively after resolving the main conflict. After a laborious set of levels, *Flower* erupted in the fast-paced, colorful rebirth of a deadened, gray-scale city and then concluded. *Journey*'s denouement is even more dramatic and far more sentimental. Near the mountain's summit, in the snow, progress becomes more and more difficult. Pace slows, then stops. My character, red hood now gray with the crust of ice, succumbs to the cold earth. The screen goes white.

Then, suddenly, the mysterious white godmother appears and looks over me. What she does remains ambiguous: some will say she resurrects me, others will claim my spirit is ejected into eternity, and still others will interpret the last scene as a final bodily hallucination. But through whirlwinds and cloth banners and the bright cobalt of sun and snow and dawn, I rush up to the summit. Who can resist the exhilaration? It's invigorating, like a cold winter wind on flushed cheeks.

When they speak about their games, the thatgamecompany crew often express a hope that they might explore or arouse positive emotions in their players, emotions they do not feel from other sorts of games. Isn't this sense of delight and vitality precisely what they are after? Yes, to be sure. But it is also the thrill of all victories, and the vertigo of all dizzinesses. Chen, Santiago, and, later, their *Journey* collaborator Robin Hunicke sell themselves short with this trite incantation about emotions. For their journey has not been one of creating *outcomes* but of culturing a *style,* an aesthetic that defines the experience without need for their aphorisms. Instead: the sand and the ruins. The wind and the fabric. The silence of a cryptographic mythology. The vertigo of breeze, the swish of dunes.

For my part, I plodded through the snow near the summit of *Journey*'s cleft mountain with another traveler, one who entered that scene with a regal scarf flowing far behind, easily twice as long as my own. We stumbled up the mountain together, cowering behind stone tablets to avoid the wind. At one point, I hobbled out foolishly before one of the game's serpentine flying enemies, who dove and sent us flying back. The impact eviscerated most of his scarf, and I felt guilty.

We took our final slog through the dense snow and thick wind, and we both collapsed together under its weight. Thinking back, I elongate the short moment before the game interrupted me with its cloying samsaric angel, and I imagine that this fallen other was Jenova or Kellee rather than some stranger, that they had allowed me to join them on their journey to journeyman. Before the screen goes white I imagine whispering my tiny counsel in the hope that they might yet reach mastery: *This. This is enough.*

3

The Blue Shell Is Everything That's Wrong with America

Putting the lie to *Mario Kart*'s even playing field

"The Blue Shell is everything that's wrong with America."

OK, nobody said that, but you can imagine someone having done so. The Blue Shell steals progress from a rightfully earned win on behalf of the lazy and the incompetent. The Blue Shell wrests spoils from leaders' fingers just as they reach for the laurel. The Blue Shell is the cruel tax of gaming, the welfare queen of kart racing. God damn you kids today. We used to have to *win* a race to win it.

I'm talking about *Mario Kart,* of course, whose Spiny Blue Shell power-up has taunted players since its second iteration in 1996–97. It's the pickup sometimes given to players far behind in a race, which homes in on the leader, bringing delight to the inferior player and torment to the superior one. Just as you were about to cross the finish, there's a Blue Shell, spinning you out so that Mario or Donkey Kong crosses just ahead of you. And, conversely, just as you thought yourself too far behind to catch up, there's a Blue Shell to help put you on the winners' podium.

1996 is a long time ago—two decades, more or less. In some sense, metaphorical though it may be, that makes the Blue Shell an adult. A lot has changed in those years. When *Mario Kart 64* first appeared, the Amazon.com IPO had not yet taken place. Bill Clinton was starting his second term as president. Mark Zuckerberg was planning his bar mitzvah. You probably didn't

< 22 >

have a mobile phone, but you might have had an AOL account. The Macarena was a thing, as was the SEGA Saturn. It's easy to forget, to lump today's Blue Shell in with yesterday's like you'd lump today's Internet in with yesterday's, forgetting that yesterday was an entire lifetime ago.

While all of us refer to the Blue Shell as such, it's actually called "Spiny's Shell" in the *Mario Kart 64* manual. This difference makes a difference, because it reconnects the shell's name to its origins and its function. A Spiny is a quadrupedal Koopa with a spiked shell. They've been around as long as the original NES *Super Mario Bros.* Back then, they served as the ammunition of Lakitu—that begoggled, cloud-riding Koopa who hurls them from the air in some overworld levels. Spiny shells are red, and thanks to their spikes they cannot be jumped atop to defeat or bumped from below to flip on their backs as can an ordinary Koopa. Only a fireball wrought by a Fire Flower–emblazoned Mario brother can defeat the Spinies—or a hero emboldened by the temporary immunity of an invincibility Star (or maybe a kicked Koopa shell, but such a resource is unlikely in the barren wastelands where Lakitu rears his head, at least in the original *SMB*).

The Spiny Shell is the most profoundly existentialist element of the Mario canon. It disrupts the entire logic of this familiar fantasy universe. We were told we could jump on things to destroy them! We were told we could flip them asunder! But no—all promises are tentative, even in the Mushroom Kingdom. Spiky Shells are chaos, unfairness, injustice. For those of us who were kids when *Super Mario Bros.* arrived, the Spiky Shell taught a lesson, and the lesson was: you are alone in the universe. Enough with your childish expectations. This is the real world, and just when you think you've mastered it, it'll pull the rug out from under you. You have to find your own way.

The blueness of Blue Shells comes from elsewhere—half a decade but an entire generation later. A Koopa Troopa with a blue shell first appeared in *Super Mario World,* the launch title for the Super Nintendo in 1990–91. Blue-backed Koopas move faster than their blue- or red-clad brethren. *Super Mario World* also marks the introduction of Yoshi, and ingesting a Blue Shell immediately causes the dinosaur steed to sprout wings and fly. Some things come easy.

The Blue Shell didn't appear again in a traditional Nintendo platformer until the triumphant return in 2006 of 2-D Mario, in *New Super Mario Bros.* for the Nintendo DS. Here, the Blue Shell takes the same form as it had sixteen years earlier, but as a power-up for the benefit of our heroes. Collecting the Blue Shell turns Mario into Shell Mario. By ducking, he becomes invulnerable under his azure armor. Shell Mario can also perform a "shell dash," enacting the familiar destructive power of a Koopaless shell sent flying by foot, but under the control of the player via his plumberly counterpart.

In contrast to the Spiky Shell—a hazard that strips certainty and authority from the player—the Blue Shell has always been associated with speed, power, and security. Despite its rarity, the Blue Shell is a conservative bonus, a feature that entrenches the comforts of Mario, Luigi, and their human pilots rather than wresting it away. Would it be too much to say that Spiky Shell was a Gen Xer's lament, an NES-bred slacker's plaid, tortugal sigh, while Blue Shell was a Gen Y transitional object, a comfort blanket—blue with calm like Linus van Pelt's—that proffers assurance to the SNES milksop every time, no matter how infrequently it might appear? Probably so.

No matter, when the two forms merge in *Mario Kart 64*, those forces struggle against each other. Chaos and comfort, futility and control all bound together in blasphemous profanity. You see, the original Blue Shell didn't just seek out the leader, not back in 1996 it didn't. Things were stranger then, less certain, less predictable. Save for the leader, any player was eligible to receive the Blue Shell. But when fired, it would first speed away like a normal shell, susceptible to any obstacle that might destroy it, whether friend or foe. After a few moments, it begins following the track, destroying anything in its path on its way to its final target: the race leader. But during this pursuit, drivers in the Blue Shell's path who hear its banshee's wail can dodge out of the way, avoiding calamity for the moment, at least.

In *Mario Kart 64,* the Blue Shell reveals both sides of its split personality: the chaos of an indifferent universe is embodied in the first few moments of prospective squandering, while the comforting dominion appears in its certain destruction of the leader. In between, red spiny indifference and blue comfort blend into an invisible violet: power actuates and squeals its siren but remains inherently impotent, easily outwitted by a well-timed dodge. The universe may not care, but that very unconcern can be focused, leveraged.

But perhaps most poetically, in *Mario Kart 64* the Blue Shell punishes hubris. A player who happens to collect a Blue Shell and store it until reaching the leader's position is rewarded only with woe. After teasing the thrower with its initial straight shot, the shell reverses course and strikes the unsuspecting leader. Perhaps one goes a step too far in reading allegory into a Mushroom Kingdom–themed kart racing game, but surely we can all marvel at the fact that 1996 still believed that an arrogant winner could be hoist on his own petard.

By 2003 everything had changed, and not just in the Mushroom Kingdom. The dot-com crash had come and gone. We blogged now, and we Googled. PlayStation 2 and Xbox had stolen the thunder from the cute, cubical GameCube, on which *Mario Kart: Double Dash!!* made its appearance.

The eager double-exclamation in its name underscores how desperate for attention and approval *Mario Kart* had become. It was willing to do anything for our love. Those of us who had cut our teeth on Lakitu's rage were too old to care about Mario ourselves and too young to have kids with whom to start caring again. We'd made and lost fortunes by then, we'd E*Traded YHOO, we'd gone to war for no reason. For their part, the former SNES tots were now adolescents interested in a different kind of magic mushroom, screeching through Liberty City rather than prancing across Donut Plains.

Here, amid the despair of longing, the Blue Shell gave up, taking on the familiar form we know to this day. In *Mario Kart: Double Dash!!,* racers in fourth place or worse can receive the item as a pickup. Wings allow it to fly rather than glide past obstacles and other drivers on its inevitable race to the would-be victor. While some hazard still faces middle-field drivers who might happen into its lofty path, such accidents are newly rare. Dejected, the Blue Shell now hisses instead of wailing its earlier klaxon. Even it doesn't want to be here. There is only shame underneath the cover of a Blue Shell.

This shame entrenched for a decade. Through *Mario Kart DS,* through *Mario Kart Wii,* through *Mario Kart 7.* In the latter, the Blue Shell was even stripped of its wings, although inexplicably it can still fly—a cruel illogic meant to wrest its last faculty from its brainless husk. And with the release of *Mario Kart 8* for Wii U, the Blue Shell's impotent entrenchment is only further affirmed by an insulting Band-Aid. A new item, the Super Horn, allows the leader to destroy the Blue Shell en route. But so rare is this pickup that some reviewers reported having seen it only once, if at all, during the game's entire campaign. Victory and defeat are just lies told out of two sides of the same mouth.

This is the Blue Shell of collapse, the Blue Shell of financial crisis, the Blue Shell of the New Gilded Age. This is the Blue Shell in Facebook blue, where anything you'd do with it already will have been done anyway on your behalf without you knowing it. To lead or to fall behind, to turn the tables or to evade one's fated fortune, these are just roles we play. Really the decision has already been made, as if by barrels in a slot machine preordained by cosmic odds tables. Gone is the chaos where once terror and comfort intertwined like smoke and sex in the darkness, where all options seemed possible even if some seemed less likely. Some hope remained, that a world of uncertainty might still afford tactics even as it also eluded them. That outcomes hadn't already been determined on our behalf behind closed doors or in data centers.

Today, winner and loser alike know that the real winners aren't even in the game, aren't even on the course. Real winners need not even bother with *Mario Kart,* for they have managed to master a real Blue Shell in the interim, a trump card against the universe. The same week the newbies and the nostalgic and the neotenous powered up their Wii U's for the first time in months to pilot cartoon apes and dinosaurs once more in *Mario Kart 8,* Sergey Brin launched his prototype Google Autonomous Car. He's already turned all of Mountain View into one big, real-world kart race—and he's coming for your town, too. How charming that you would pilot toy cars in mimicry of the future.

For its part, Nintendo is more like us than it is like Google. As of *Mario Kart 8*'s release, it needed a Blue Shell more than anyone. Hemorrhaging money, the company punctuated a year of disappointing sales by flubbing the launch of the life simulator *Tomodachi Life* in the West by making only heterosexual relationships possible—failing to notice that those NES and SNES kids of yore are now adults and that they might just as well like Daisy to be Peach's prince. Its last-ditch effort would count as irony if it weren't so tragic: the *Mario Kart 8* Limited Edition Set. Those who preordered or raced to retail on day one received a box with the game and a Spiny Blue Shell collectible, a molded plastic trophy celebrating the futile dream of victory and the final incarceration of chaos. At long last, both victory and defeat can be definitively brought to a halt, forever suspended in inaction. There, the Blue Shell Participation Trophy overlooks the gray pavement of your cubicle—if you're lucky enough to have one—where, like *Mario Kart* players of every generation, you labor quietly under the false impression that someday you too will be a victor.

4

Little Black Sambo, I'm Going to Eat You Up!

What a game made to understand thousands of words reveals about language

5th Cell's Nintendo DS game *Scribblenauts* features an enormous dictionary of terms, any of which can be written to summon objects to solve puzzles in the game. Just about anything you might want to write, from "acai berry" to "zygote," gets transformed into a functional object. With well over twenty thousand words represented, some are bound to be surprising. And indeed, shortly after its release, a player found and reported an unusual term in the game's dictionary: "sambo."[1]

If you don't know it already, *sambo* is a racial slur that originated in eighteenth-century British and American English. It was (and remains) a derogatory way to refer to a black man. While its origins remain somewhat mysterious, the term is best known today thanks to the late nineteenth-century children's book *The Story of Little Black Sambo,* which tells the story of Black Mumbo and Black Jumbo and their boy Little Black Sambo, who outwits a series of tigers who threaten, "I'm going to eat you up!"[2]

The cultural context for *Little Black Sambo* is complex. Its author, Helen Bannerman, was a Scottish expatriate living in Madras during the period of British colonization. This explains both the presence of tigers and the "blackness" of the boy, since the British often referred to South Asians as "black." Yet the name she chose referred then, as it does now, to a largely American term

< 28 >

for African slaves. While the original edition caricatured Southern Indian appearances, later editions, including those published in the United States, depicted Sambo as a "darky" or a minstrel golliwogg, further cementing the negative racial association of a negro simpleton. By the 1930s the *Little Black Sambo* character appeared regularly in popular culture, including animation adaptations of Bannerman's story. In a 1935 animated cartoon that bears the title *Little Black Sambo,* for example, the characters are clearly meant to refer to African American blackness, as the addition of the black mammy and stereotypical speech suggest.

But by this time, negative reaction to the story and the figure of black Sambo were already beginning to appear. As the years passed, many began criticizing the book as offensive to black children, and it gradually fell out of favor in libraries and schools, even as other editions appeared that attempted to rescue the story from its racist roots. (Among these is the 1996 *The Story of Little Babaji,* a direct copy of Bannerman's original text with new illustrations by Fred Marcellino. This edition became a best seller, and Marcellino was credited with rescuing the tale from its accidental fate as a symbol of American racism.)

Given a century of racial baggage, one can see why it would be surprising to discover that *Scribblenauts* recognizes *sambo* at all. But the game does much more than just recognize terms: it translates each typed word into an object with different properties and behaviors.

Entering the word *sambo* produces what appears to be a watermelon on-screen. And, alas, the watermelon too has a long history of African American stereotyping, making the inclusion of *sambo* seem even more racially motivated. The connection between African Americans and watermelon seems to have originated in emancipated slaves' post–Civil War cultivation practices. As the historian William Black explains:

> Free black people grew, ate, and sold watermelons, and in doing so made the fruit a symbol of their freedom.

> Southern whites, threatened by blacks' newfound free-
> dom, responded by making the fruit a symbol of black
> people's perceived uncleanliness, laziness, childishness,
> and unwanted public presence. This racist trope then
> exploded in American popular culture, becoming so per-
> vasive that its historical origin became obscure.[3]

All told, it's easy to understand why a player who, curious at the depth of the game's dictionary or bored with more ordinary terms, happened to type "sambo" into *Scribblenauts* might come to the reasonable conclusion that the game's creators didn't intend to insert a subtle racist commentary into an otherwise wholesome and harmless children's game.

Yet it wasn't intended to be. In an interview, *Scribblenauts* creative director Jeremiah Slaczka insisted that neither his game nor his company is racist.[4] And I believe him, partly because he also admitted that he had no idea what *sambo* meant, let alone that the term had a history. According to 5th Cell, they included *sambo* because it is also a Spanish term for a type of gourd that grows on the chilacayote plant, one that rather resembles a wa-termelon. Apparently the watermelon-like graphic was simply re-used for the sambo, a necessary strategy when one must literalize tens of thousands of different terms in a videogame.

The most interesting feature of the *Scribblenauts* sambo fi-asco is not that it offers evidence that 5th Cell (or some rogue agent within it) wishes to make negative racial comments about African Americans by sneaking a slur into a game, nor that the term didn't get vetted and removed before launch, nor that 5th Cell didn't issue an earnest apology, even if its publisher Warner Bros. Interactive eventually did. No, the interesting part is that Slaczka *didn't know what "sambo" meant in the first place.* Or more precisely, what that ignorance signifies.

This unfamiliarity turns out to be a common one. Reading the comments on stories about the controversy on game enthusiast websites like *Kotaku* and *Joystiq*, or the many forum discussions on fan sites like *NeoGaf*, it becomes clear that a great many people—or, at least, a great many enthusiasts of videogames—aren't familiar with *sambo* at all.[5]

It's not for any lack of history. While cartoons like the animation cited above would never reach the airwaves today, the figure of Sambo did last far beyond the 1930s. Perhaps most notably, Sambo's was the name of a chain of family restaurants, similar to Denny's, which thrived from 1957 to 1982. The name started innocuously enough: Sam Battistone and Newell Bohnett founded the original restaurant in Santa Barbara (the only one that remains) and combined parts of their names (*Sam* + *Bo*hnett) to create Sambo's. The two quickly realized the association with *Little Black Sambo*, and given the popularity of the book and the character they decorated the restaurants with scenes from its pages. The restaurant was well-known, popular, and everywhere, boasting twelve hundred locations in forty-seven states by the late 1970s.

If you read the coverage and conversations attached to the revelation of "sambo" in *Scribblenauts*, many players—particularly those previously unfamiliar with the term—suggest that the very idea of discussing the inclusion of this word in the game is ludicrous. Some slough off the situation as an unfortunate but unimportant accident.[6] Some deny the very existence of racial significance in the situation.[7] Some suggest that the coverage itself enacts racial violence by reintroducing an "obscure" (to them, anyway) slur back into the common imagination.[8] Some even accuse the coverage itself of logocentrism, angry that the Spanish sense of a word might be subjugated to the English one.[9] In all these cases, a common attitude prevails: this is not a big deal. It is a distraction, and it deserves only limited attention. "Sambo," this attitude holds, is just a word.

But here's the problem: *Scribblenauts* is a game about words. Indeed, it is a game about very many words and their relative uniqueness. This makes its case different from earlier examples of similar types of accidental intolerance in videogames. The year before 5th Cell's blunder, Sony delayed the anticipated user-creation platformer game *Little Big Planet* after discovering "potentially offensive" lyrics from the Koran in a background song.[10] And shortly before the release of *Scribblenauts*, players and critics debated whether the adventure game *Shadow Complex* should be boycotted because it was based on the science fictional worlds of Orson Scott Card, an outspoken critic of same-sex marriage.[11] In these situations, the potentially offensive payload the games carried were secondary to their intended expression and purpose. But such is not the case with *Scribblenauts* and the watermelon. It is a game about what words mean and do when mustered in particular situations. Indeed, its puzzles are mundane and uninteresting, until new terms alight upon them. In *Scribblenauts*, every word draws attention to itself, by necessity and by design.

We might conclude that *Scribblenauts* is a game whose very goal is to make us think about the words people utter, and responses we expect. In this sense, the discourse *Scribblenauts'* *sambo* produces is *precisely the purpose of the game*. It is a game meant to make us think and rethink our words, their uses, and their implicit behavior. And the outcry and confusion shows that it was successful.

What sense, then, might we make of *sambo*? The idea that this slur has lost much of its sense startles me. Even as a player in my early thirties at the time of the game's release, I remember reading *Little Black Sambo* as a kid. I remember going to Sambo's restaurant. I remember being both charmed and disturbed by both. When I consider that the idea might have fallen so far into disuse as to disappear, two feelings well up in me.

On the one hand, it is tempting to celebrate this new ignorance, as some players suggest. If a more accepting and less bigoted society is one we want to live in, then there is some sign of cultural success when a racial slur obsolesces. But on the other hand, this very neglect points to a social ill even worse than racism itself: disavowal. We must strive for more than the destruction of stereotype, slur, and other visible signs of bigotry, as if eliminating the symptoms also cures the cause.

Barack Obama's now-famous speech on racism during the 2008 election was smart and moving not because it resolved anything about race in America but because it acknowledged the thorny tangle that arises when we think and talk about race—and when we don't.[12] Anger and resentment and fear on both sides, on all sides. Obama called it a *stalemate*, a deadlock that can be overcome only by trying something new rather than issuing new helpings of blame and praise, opportunity and concession. In the land of videogames, our battles are usually much lowlier. They are fictional, and fantastic, and ultimately unimportant. Often we have to work very hard to find meaning in such works and our experiences of them, struggling to shout above the din of conversations about politics and literature and economics and film and art to make our work appear to have even a trifle of relevance.

Yet, when such matters are thrust on us by happenstance, what do we do? We resist. We repudiate. "It's just a game," we say. "Don't ruin my experience." But an alternative ought to occur to us: *what if this is the experience*? What if messy quandaries about the ambiguity of *sambo* is precisely the sort of thing that *Scribblenauts* was meant to bring us? Then we'd have to face an uncomfortable muddle. Far from having played itself out in our hearts and our streets, racism remains, visible of course, but also hidden among the words we use and the ones we don't. There it lies, unflinching, waiting to discovered by accident in a videogame, like a secret found in a box in the attic years later.

5

Can a Gobbler Have It All?

Why *Ms. Pac-Man* is the ultimate—or at least the first—feminist videogame

Looking at the two cabinets side by side, it would be tempting to think that *Ms. Pac-Man* is merely a sequel, a follow-up to the immensely successful 1980 original. The marquee typography is the same, the cabinet of a similar style, and, of course, the games look and sound like they are variations on a theme.

But *Ms. Pac-Man* was not a sequel, not in the ordinary fashion, anyway. It was really what we'd call a *modification* or a *mod* today, although we have to be careful ascribing modern concepts to the recent past; in the early 1980s, "mods" didn't exist. To get a sense of how *Ms. Pac-Man* came about, you need to understand something about two topics: coin-op platforms and arcade enhancement kits.

By 1980 several standardized, interchangeable cartridge home platforms had already been introduced, such as the Atari VCS, the Mattel Intellivision, and the Fairchild Channel F. These platforms were created with the intention of playing many different games on the same hardware. By contrast, coin-ops—the popular way to play videogames at the time—were one-off design affairs, machines that played one game only. Even though each cabinet was capable of playing only one game in those early years, platform thinking had actually begun very early in the life of coin-ops.

For example, Kee Games' popular 1974 title *Tank* was inspired by 1972's *PONG* in more ways than just the creative influence of a

< 34 >

fledgling new industry. To get around certain regulatory issues affecting cash-based businesses at the time, and to make the games market appear larger, Atari founder Nolan Bushnell recruited his friend Joe Keenan to helm a wholly owned subsidiary that would appear to be a competitor. Kee Games managed to "hire away" key Atari engineer Steve Bristow, who "borrowed" his own approach to projectile physics from previous Atari games in implementing *Tank*. Later, Atari reabsorbed Kee Games and reincorporated its ideas. Among them, the Atari VCS pack-in title *Combat* was based on *Tank*.

Even if *Tank* and *PONG* didn't share the same computational infrastructure, they suggested the idea that multiple games could be made from a common architecture. Even if it wasn't expressly designed to be multipurpose, once a coin-op architecture was created and manufactured, it only made sense to consider using it for other games.

Like all coin-ops, *Pac-Man* had its own custom computational design, including some pretty advanced features compared with home consoles of the time: a Zilog Z80 served as the CPU, mated to 2K RAM, and the game occupied 16K of ROM. The game was built to support eight 16 × 16 pixel sprites and sixteen colors.

As a list of specifications these statistics are meaningless, but infrastructural details can help us understand what it means for a game to be what it is. For example, *Pac-Man*'s video display supports a resolution of 224 × 228 pixels, split into a 28 × 36 grid of "characters" of 8 × 8 pixels each. In *Pac-Man*'s case, a character is not a letter or number but a bitmap tile. In some cases, a character comprises a single in-game entity, like a dot, and in other cases, multiple characters form a single logical object on-screen, like a cherry.

Given this framework, we can also think of *Pac-Man* as a potential platform with certain capabilities. As it happens, the buggy racing game *Rally X* was built on the same architecture as *Pac-Man* (both games were made by Namco), although the display is rotated 90 degrees into a horizontal position. Even as early

as 1980, coin-op boards and cabinet assemblies were already embracing standardization and reuse.

But one of the most popular mechanisms for coin-op reuse
didn't take place entirely in the hands of developers. A coin-op is
a major investment, not just for the developer but also for the operator. It costs thousands of dollars and, more importantly, takes
up valuable space in a bowling alley or arcade. Maximizing coin-
drop—the amount of quarters a machine could claim—became a
priority for a proprietor of an arcade venue. Today, when players
tire of a particular game, they can just buy a new title affordably
or download a new one for free. But for a coin-op owner, such a
circumstance would have required replacing an entire cabinet.

Enhancement kits were developed to address this problem.
These additional chips or board assemblies attached to an arcade
machine and gave it a new behavior. Some enhancement kits included major changes like new graphics or behavior, while others offered small tune-ups, like new high score behavior or faster,
more challenging operation. One *Asteroids* enhancement kit, for
example, extends the number of digits available in the scores.

Enhancement kits took the form of raw boards or components,
but they were relatively easy for arcade operators to install. For
the *Asteroids* kit just mentioned, the operator simply removed
the 6502 CPU chip from the *Asteroids* board, inserted the 6502
CPU chip into the daughter card that contains the enhancement
programming, and then plugged the daughter card back into the
vacated 6502 CPU socket on the game's main board. Arcade operators already accessed the guts of their machines to claim coins or
perform maintenance, so enhancement kits were a welcome, af-
fordable way to extend the life of a cabinet investment. Increased
difficulty was a common use of enhancement kits, since they offered a way to refresh an aging game cabinet, drawing users who'd
mastered the game back into it. This was especially useful if you
had only a few cabinets in a venue where the same people might
often gather, such as a bowling alley or a tavern.

A less well-known *Pac-Man* sequel, 1981's *Pac-Man Plus,* is really just an enhancement kit for the original. It speeds up the game's overall play and changes the maze color. In addition, all the fruit is updated, and when eaten some of the ghosts disappear. At other times, the maze walls disappear, too. In addition to the integrated circuits needed to update the game on the inside, the *Pac-Man Plus* enhancement kit also included a new marquee for the cabinet to signal that this was a new kind of *Pac-Man*.

Ms. Pac-Man was originally conceived as an enhancement kit, not as an entirely new game. But there was a wrinkle: it was an *unauthorized* enhancement kit, created by fans. And not just fans, but MIT hardware geek fans. Intrigued at the prospect of altering arcade games as a hobby, two students named Doug Macrae and Kevin Curran started messing around with coin-op boards. They eventually started a company called General Computing Corporation (GCC) to sell these wares. (GCC would go on to more elaborate computer hardware efforts. The company designed the Atari 7800 home console, the Apple Personal Laser Printer, and the Mac HyperDrive, an internal hard disk for the original Mac.)

One of GCC's popular boards was *Super Missile Attack,* an enhancement board for the popular 1980 coin-op title *Missile Command.* The board added different colors and a new attract mode; more, faster missiles and clouds that get smaller as the game progresses (a benefit because it would also increase the profit from an individual cabinet); a new attacker, the UFO, which moves faster and more randomly than ordinary planes and satellites and fires a deadly new "Laser" weapon; and new sounds, such that a seemingly familiar game could signal that it was "new and improved" from across the bar or arcade.

These third-party enhancement kits were possible only because Atari and other coin-op manufacturers published detailed electronics schematics for their games, presumably for repair purposes. Thanks to these schematics, folks like Macrae and Curran were able to understand the hardware configuration of popular games and plan improvements.

The software, however, had to be entirely reverse engineered. It was usually done with microprocessor emulation that allowed enhancement hackers to stop the game in progress at any time and examine the state of memory or program registers, facilitating changes to the program bit-by-bit. Thanks partly to the complexity of the process, most enhancement kits involved relatively small alterations to the game, requiring changes to a small fraction of the overall code base.

Macrae and Curran managed to get a *Pac-Man* board and wondered what they could do with it. Like *Missile Command,* the game was enormously popular, and thus it made a good target for an enhancement kit. The two devised a new game based on *Pac-Man,* which they called *Crazy Otto.* The game looked remarkably similar to *Pac-Man,* with notable changes in the sprites and mazes. Crazy Otto himself had a body much like *Pac-Man's* titular gobbler, but attached to a pair of awkward, lanky legs.

GCC made four major changes to *Pac-Man* in the *Crazy Otto* design, changes that anyone who has played *Ms. Pac-Man* will immediately recognize as exactly the ones that distinguish the game from its apparent predecessor.

First, the game had four different mazes, all in unique colors, to break up the monotony of the game. Second, the behavior of the monsters that chase the player hero was altered. *Pac-Man's* monsters look like they are chasing you, but each one actually deployed a relatively simple, deterministic logic. When considered in concert with specific *Pac-Man* movement, one could even memorize a fixed path around the maze, a technique described in various strategy guides. *Crazy Otto* introduced different and less predictable monster behavior, which couldn't be counteracted with memorized paths through the maze. Third, the bonus fruits were made to bounce around the maze rather than appear in one location. And fourth, the game includes narrative "intermissions" between certain levels. The intermission showed a female Otto (her name was Anna) chasing the male around the screen. The enhancement was accomplished by replacing one of *Pac-Man's*

ROM boards with a new board and altering the program code such that accessing specific addresses would branch the main program flow to the new auxiliary board.

GCC thought the game played well. But thanks to the terms of a settlement agreement with Atari in a multimillion-dollar lawsuit the larger company had filed over the *Missile Command* enhancement kit, the company was obliged not to publish enhancement kits without manufacturer permission.[1] So GCC contacted Midway, which had the North American rights to *Pac-Man*.

Things proceeded quickly. GCC first showed *Crazy Otto* to Midway in mid-October 1981. By the end of the month, the parties had signed a contract and added Midway's logo to the game's attract mode. Otto was long gone by now; this was a *Pac-Man* game. But sometime in November, Midway suggested that the player character be changed to a woman.[2] With lipstick, eyelashes, a beauty mark, and a bow in her hair (or where her hair would be, anyway—although an earlier version of the Ms. Pac-Man sprite featured a full head of flowing red locks).[3] Women, it turned out, loved *Pac-Man,* and Midway theorized that making the main character female would only accelerate the game's certain success.[4]

As for the game's title, nobody knows exactly how it came about. *Miss Pac-Man* was the working title for some time, although the obviously unworkable *Pac-Woman* was also considered. At some point, Midway executives apparently worried that a *Miss* Pac-Man couldn't have a baby without raising eyebrows (Pac-Man Jr. is delivered in the third intermission), and so the title was altered to *Mrs. Pac-Man.*[5] The change to "Ms." apparently happened at the last minute. There are apocryphal reports that agitation from a Midway employee, gender unspecified, underwrote the new title, but we may never know for sure.

What we do know is this: the genesis of *Ms. Pac-Man* recalls both traditional and progressive models of the role of women.

From the perspective of tradition, *Ms. Pac-Man*'s formation from *Pac-Man* is almost biblical in its implications. Here's how

the Old Testament explains the creation of woman from the rib
man:

> And Jehovah God caused a deep sleep to fall on the man,
> and he slept. And he took one of his ribs [tselah], and
> closed up the flesh underneath. And Jehovah God formed
> the rib which he had taken from the man [adam] into a
> woman ['isshah], and brought her to the man. And the
> man said, This now at last is bone of my bones, and flesh
> of my flesh. For this shall be called woman ['isshah], be-
> cause this has been taken from out of man ['ish]. (Genesis
> 2:21–23)

A *tsela'* is a rib, but also a side, a plank—a board, even. Man (*adam*)
refers to humankind, the man that god created, as yet undefined
in terms of gender. From this, God's action creates man (*ish*) and
woman (*isshah*). From a common origin comes two distinct iterations of the same prototype.

I'm not just trying to play a clever philologist's game here.
The analogy of Genesis helps explain how to think about *Pac-
Man* and *Ms. Pac-Man* in a structural way, albeit one that's also
immensely and conveniently poetic given their relation to each
other. Without hyperbole, one can say that *Ms. Pac-Man* was created from the rib—or at least the board—of *Pac-Man*, but in reverse, a chip removed, a new daughterboard added.

Both games are instances of a more common underlying structure, and that structure makes both of them possible, individually
and together. The *adam* of the system is the platform, the abstraction of integrated circuits that makes games like these possible.
Understanding this layer of both games is related to but distinct
from understanding each individually.

But even as *Ms. Pac-Man* is allegorically suggestive of the very
first account of woman in the Judeo-Christian tradition, it also
embraces and performs the new progressivism; a gobbler who can
have it all.

Such a claim seems preposterous on first blush, especially if you consider the narrative exposition of Ms. Pac-Man and her relation to the hero of the original game. It seems entirely gender normative and wholly traditional. In the first intermission, "Act 1—They Meet," Pac-Man is chased by Inky while Ms. Pac-Man is chased by Blinky. The ghosts bang heads, the Pac-Persons escape, and a heart appears between them. In "Act 2—The Chase," Pac-Man and Ms. Pac-Man chase each other quickly across the screen five times, with more speed each time. And in "Act 3—Junior," a stork drops off a bundle containing a tiny Pac-Man.

But this 1950s gender role performance stands in stark opposition to the game's paratexts. Sell-sheets for *Ms. Pac-Man* depicted the game's heroine decked out in a lurid fur, emerging in the misty night from a chauffeured, classic Rolls Royce or Deusenberg. At the top the sell-sheet reads "Introducing . . . the new femme fatale of the game world."

Which is it? Is Ms. Pac-Man a demure housewife and mother, won over by Pac-Man before retiring to the duties of uxorial traditionalism? Or is she a vampy seductress, a femme fatale slinking out at night to lure quarters from the pockets of unassuming, anonymous "patrons?" Could there be two more incompatible pictures of a character than these? Perhaps the *Ms.* in the game's title offers the key to reconciling the two sides of our gobbler heroine.

"Ms." was used as early as the seventeenth century as an abbreviation for the formal honorific "Mistress," which is the unabbreviated version of both Mrs. and Miss, although we tend not to use it because of its primary meaning of "paramour or courtesan."[6] It was revived in the early 1950s, as a possible convenience in writing business letters. By the 1960s, Sheila Michaels suggested the term for "a title for a woman who did not belong to a man," based on a typographical error from a piece of mail her roommate had received.[7] But during the civil rights era of the 1960s, there was not yet enough of an audience for suggestions of gender equity for the term to catch on.

It took until the early 1970s for the concept to take off. Michaels made the suggestion again in a 1971 radio interview, which a friend of Gloria Steinem heard. It became the title of Steinem's new magazine (*Ms.*). But more importantly, Ms. was advanced in practice all throughout the 1970s, as women entered the workforce in larger numbers and as women's lib advanced.

Ms. introduces a logic of ambiguity, ambiguity of a very specific type. It decouples a woman's professional life from her personal one. And this is just the ambiguity that is performed in *Ms. Pac-Man.*

For one part, Ms. Pac-Man is a coquettish seductress, enticing players to drop their coins and try to conquer her. For another part, Ms. Pac-Man is a working girl. She is, after all, the first female lead in a videogame. Everything Pac-Man can do, she can do—and better. Her job is less predictable and more exciting, making it more challenging and rewarding. And yet Ms. Pac Man is a traditionalist, a family woman willing to make a home with the right man—one whom she chases as much as he chases her—and a mother, able and willing to care for her Pac-progeny. These two worlds are separated in the game, the mechanical domain of gameplay and the narrative domain of interlude. Moreover, it is the challenges of work that bring the two Pacs together, their common struggle against the foes that are the game's monsters.

Another kind of ambiguity is the professional circumstance out of which *Ms. Pac-Man* itself emerged—an unauthorized hack made into an official sequel, one that would better the original in every way.

And finally, *Ms. Pac-Man* embraces the culture of the tavern, the arcade, the bowling alley—those great third spaces of the 1960s and 1970s—at exactly the time when women's lib was really taking hold. Far from being just Pac-Man in a bow, Ms. Pac-Man offers a counterpoint to the very idea of feminine roles in the videogame experience. And in the arcade, too: she upset the idea that women were mere accessories or playthings in the arcade, as was so commonly seen on coin-op sell-sheets for games like

Gotcha and *Computer Space,* which featured scantily clad women bent or draped over videogame cabinets.

This ambiguity has remained in force as *Ms. Pac-Man* has moved from videogame to pop culture icon. Search your favorite online retailer and you'll find demure, pink Ms. Pac-Man baby bibs alongside racy Ms. Pac-Man lingerie. She is capable of supporting both these roles, and everything in between.

Ms. Pac-Man is perhaps the apotheosis of the feminist videogame, structurally, mechanically, fictionally, and temporally. It is a work about a woman who triumphs over a man by playing his game better than he ever could, about one who wins over millions by being more challenging rather than simpler, who keeps her heels and celebrates her feminine curves—or perhaps I should say curve—who is willing to woo and to be wooed, who balances being a professional, a wife, and a mother, all without compromising any one of her desires.

6

Racketeer Sports

The real moral danger of videogames isn't violence,
it's swindling

On April 20, 1999, Eric Harris and Dylan Klebold had murdered
thirteen students and injured twenty-three others at Columbine
High School before taking their own lives. In the months after
the massacre, violent videogames were cited over and over again
as a possible, if not likely, factor in the duo's killing spree. In a
2000 article on "video games and aggressive thoughts, feelings,
and behavior," the psychologists Craig A. Anderson and Karen
E. Dill seemed to relish their good fortune of having a massacre to lead their story. "One possible contributing factor," the
two wrote of Columbine, "is violent video games. Harris and
Klebold enjoyed playing the bloody, shoot-'em-up video game
Doom, a game licensed by the U.S. military to train soldiers to
effectively kill."[1]

Talking points like these have appeared again and again in
sound bite detractions of videogames. After Adam Lanza gunned
down twenty children and six staff members at Sandy Hook
Elementary School in late 2012, authorities began the kind of
forensic investigation reserved for airplane crashes and sites of
murderous terrorism. The details of Lanza's life become cata-
logs of potential deviances. He had made his bed that December
morning. His armoire held five matching tan shirts and five pairs
of khaki pants. An empty cereal bowl flanked damaged computer
parts on his desk. And as any veteran of America's periodic sagas

< 44 >

of horror and grief wrought by young white men would expect, the investigators duly announced they had found "thousands of dollars worth of graphically violent videogames," according to one media report, inside the Newtown home Lanza shared with his mother, whom he also killed.[2]

It was expected news. Months earlier, just after the massacre, National Rifle Association CEO Wayne LaPierre had delivered a lengthy statement on the matter in a desperate attempt to stiff-arm gun control regulation after the massacre.[3] In it, he called out "vicious, violent videogames with names like *Bulletstorm, Grand Theft Auto, Mortal Kombat,* and *Splatterhouse*" as evidence of a "callous, corrupt, and corrupting shadow industry," which was the real cause of violent slaughters like Lanza's. Television news shows fell into line and ran segments about local Newtown children voluntarily forsaking videogames. Vice President Joseph Biden established a gun violence task force, inviting media executives from film and game companies to White House briefings to answer for themselves.

Even among individuals and organizations who believe that assault weapons ought to be banned in America, shades of LaPierre's diatribe fell across leadership-class opinion like a closing curtain, the audience murmur on the last act of the indescribable mystery. Videogames made them do it. Newtown's aftermath offered yet another example of the consensus view that videogames are stimulants to the most pernicious real-world depravities imaginable, their fantasy violence cutting a hole in America's soul.

Columbine was a watershed moment in the discourse of game violence, but it was hardly the first.

In 1993 the fighting game *Mortal Kombat* had caused a moral panic over its absurdly gory depictions of hand-to-hand combat and its lethal finishing moves, called "fatalities." Partly responding to a U.S. congressional hearing about games like *Doom* and *Mortal Kombat,* the Entertainment Software Rating Board (ESRB) was established in 1994, charged to adopt, assign, and enforce age and content ratings for videogames.

And way back in 1976, *Death Race,* a coin-op driving game inspired by Paul Bartel's cult film *Death Race 2000,* inaugurated moral outrage over videogame violence. The graphics are rudimentary, but even in the mid-1970s the idea of a game in which players run cars over stick figures provoked the same media frenzy that *Doom* and *Mortal Kombat* would two decades later. Even our beloved gobbler *Pac-Man* hasn't been immune to accusations of morbid perversity: "a yellow orb with a mouth race[s] around the screen chomping up ghosts and goblins," chide Anderson and Dill in their account of this apparently grisly game.[4]

In 1983, when polite society was worried about the videogame arcade and its seedy lures, the psychologists Geoffrey R. Loftus and Elizabeth F. Loftus published *Mind at Play,* a book that attempted to explain the new phenomenon of games. Among other things, the Loftuses point out that videogames embrace *partial reinforcement,* a type of operant conditioning in which a reward is provided intermittently.[5] Partial reinforcement is the logic of B. F. Skinner's infamous behaviorist rat experiments, as well as the rationale by which casino slot machine payout schedules run. In casinos, reinforcement schedules are designed to prolong the duration of play without losing the house money over the long haul. In early video arcades, play was also discretized, and games were designed partly to maximize "coin-drop," the frequency with which an individual coin-op cabinet took receipt of a quarter and delivered a short-term play experience.

While the Loftuses have something to say about the content of games, most of their interpretive commentary feels quaint more than thirty years hence. For example, they cite *Donkey Kong,* that ur-game of the gender-normative "save the princess" design pattern considered retrograde today, as a positive example of how games "are beginning to focus on rescue instead of on destruction."[6] They are primarily interested in the structure of videogames, the way that coin-op cabinets and arcades in particular structured temptation and reward, no matter whether spaceships or monsters blipped along the screen once a game was actuated.

If it gets read at all, the Loftuses' study of games is considered out of date today, of mostly historical interest because of its focus on arcade play rather than home computer, television gaming, or handheld gaming. By the time *Doom* and *Mortal Kombat* had risen to popularity, the American video arcade had all but disappeared, save for the occasional mini-golf clubhouse and cinema lobby. Meanwhile, games had come a long way from the abstract, cartoon "violence" of *Death Race* and *Pac-Man.* A moral outrage over videogames' violent content was really only possible once that content could make reasonable claims toward realism, once games could be treated like television, another medium that has been decried for the images it depicts more than the way it structures leisure or alters the shape of ideas.

In fact, worries about television and videogame violence rehearse the same obsessions that bothered the media theorist Marshall McLuhan decades earlier: a blindness to the operation of a medium in favor of an amplification of their meanings. Videogames, which the Loftuses had tried to present as a generally positive medium whose risks mainly related to their similarities to intermittent rewards, suddenly became "murder simulators."

By the early 1990s titles like *Mortal Kombat* and events like Columbine had sealed games' fate. If games were going to be corrupt and wicked, they were going to do so in the same way as literature and film and television had been thought to do: through their content, not their form or their operation. In so doing, one of the most obvious troublesome connections between videogames and moral degeneration has been left largely unexplored and unquestioned. It's the concern that the Loftuses raised in 1983: the idea that videogames might overlap with corruption and manipulation of the type found in casino gaming. Yet to wonder whether games like *Pac-Man* or Pokémon can be legally proved to be illicit gambling or rackets prosecutable under RICO is to ask the wrong question. While legal protections from criminal manipulations are hardly irrelevant, the moral virtue or turpitude of a practice also deserves social and cultural evaluation. It amounts to asking whether videogames might have effects akin to racketeering, in addition to providing idle, harmless entertainment.

Traditionally, rackets are considered fraudulent because they offer a service that solves a problem that doesn't really exist, or that its racketeers themselves create. The classic example is the protection racket, in which an organized crime syndicate offers a shopkeeper the opportunity to pay a *pizzo* for protection against harm—harm that the protectors themselves would inflict if the protection payment is withheld. Unlike extortion, racketeering veils its coercion. It does so not only to look more legitimate but also to alter the relationship between the coerced and the coercer—effectively *making* the relationship more legitimate.

The mafioso's *pizzo* is both true and false. The demand for protection payment is artificial and contrived, coherent only within the rules of coercion that the mafioso himself has introduced by virtue of the demand for protection money in the first place. But once the relationship is established, it actually operates as a semi-legitimate protection arrangement despite its compulsory and extortive nature. The shopkeeper or business owner who keeps step with his racketeer overseers not only receives protection from the violence they might otherwise inflict but also from harm from other, rival actors who might seek to impinge on an organized crime ring's territory. The faithful shopkeeper might even enlist his extortionist's assistance in resolving conflicts or facilitating new business transactions. Criminal and guileful though extortion may be, racketeers are not grifters; they and their organizations create an actual community, even if one in which kinship is compulsory.

Even if it's fundamentally a relationship of swindling, the subject of a racket is imbued with constant ambiguity regarding the relationship's status as virtuous or vicious. Coin-op games (which have a long-standing connection to organized crime anyway, thanks to their utility as cash-only money-laundering tools) offer a similarly curious relationship. On the one hand, a coin-op game like *Pac-Man* or *Defender* demands payment with the understanding that it will do its best to eject the player from the game as quickly as possible. But on the other hand, the act of doing so creates part of the game's very structure: a challenge that the player can, through a combination of good fortune and expertise, master to the point that he or she has overcome the three-minute average play session that coin-op manufacturers hoped would yield maximum coin-drop. This is the same sensation that the slot machine player has when winning a payout—but of course, in both cases, the systems are designed such that the occasional anomaly doesn't alter the overall results of the system; the expert player and the jackpot winner are exceptions that prove the rule.

But after the fall of the coin-op arcade, we forgot about the similarities between games and racketeering. Games became a media consumable: cartridges and discs purchased like video-tapes or chewing gum. Once sold at a fixed price, the player's relationship to a game's creator and distributor was essentially severed. He or she might play all or none of the game without any further obligation of any kind. Videogames became commodities.

Then, shortly after the Columbine massacre re-entrenched the connection between games and violence, a new model of videogame delivery now known as "free-to-play" emerged. As the name suggests, free-to-play titles cost nothing, at least at the start. This model was first limited to downloadable, massively multiplayer online games (MMOs), and in particular games targeted at children who might not have the financial apparatus with which to make an online purchase. *Neopets* rose to prominence in the West, and *Maple Story* in the East. Generally speaking, these games provided the gameplay experience for free, adding the opportunity to purchase virtual items or add-ons for an extra fee—things like clothing, hairstyles, or pets for their in-game characters.

Between 2003 and 2009 two big shifts took place in the games marketplace. The first was Facebook, which released a platform for developers to make apps and games that would run within the social network's ecosystem. The second was the iPhone, the Apple App Store, and the copycats and spin-offs that it inspired. By the end of the first decade of the new millennium, free-to-play had become the norm for new games, particularly those being released for play online, via downloads, on social networks, and on smartphones—a category that is quickly overtaking disc-based games in both sales and cultural significance.

Just as casino operators, coin-op leisure machine owners, and mafiosi had come to appreciate the reliable revenues that various forms of coercion facilitate, so game developers and publishers began to see the opportunity to make far more money on individual games than they had been able to do selling them as one-off physical products.

In 2009 Zynga launched *FarmVille,* a game that would soon reach over eighty million players on Facebook. Like all free-to-play games, it offers a core experience for free, offering add-ons and features for payment via "farm cash" scrip. Players could purchase farm cash through real-money transactions, earn it through gameplay accomplishments, or receive it as a reward for completing external offers like watching video ads or signing up for unrelated services that pay referral fees to game operators. Famously, Zynga's CEO Mark Pincus sought out every possible method for increasing revenues for Zynga's games. "I knew I needed revenues, right, fucking, now. . . . I did every horrible thing in the book to, just to get revenues right away," he told attendees at a Berkeley startup mixer in 2009.[7]

Among these techniques: requiring players to stop playing after having expended in-game "energy," or to pay to replenish for immediate continued play; structuring in-game activities such that they would take far longer than any single-play session could reasonably last and requiring players to return at prescheduled intervals to complete those tasks or else risk losing work they'd previously done—and possibly spent cash money to pursue; spreading notices and demands among their Facebook friends to secure items or favors otherwise inaccessible.

The results were swift. Zynga made hundreds of millions of dollars in 2009 alone. The company began to swell with largesse, consuming smaller developers and building a new gaming empire that boiled the blood of incumbents still wedded to the hits-and-commodities model. Big game titles like *Call of Duty* and *Grand Theft Auto* might take years and hundreds of millions of dollars to develop and market, only to be subject to the commodity model of shipping disks in boxes and hoping for impressive first-week sales, just like Hollywood counts on for big tent film releases. Not to mention those games' continued association with violence and delinquency, an accusation difficult to make against a wholesome-looking, cartoonish farming game.

Individually, free-to-play transactions don't seem terribly insidious—just like coin-op games, slot machines, and *pizzo* collection don't when examined as individual, isolated acts. Paying a dollar for a virtual hat or a reprieve to retry a level doesn't seem terribly troubling. But just as coin-op cabinets structure their challenges in relation to a game that starts only to end as quickly as possible, so free-to-play games also alter the experience, and thereby the aesthetics, of games. In the worst cases, like the card-based battle game *Rage of Bahamet,* games become a "pay to win" affair, in which the players who pay the most perform the best. But even proponents of free-to-play have realized that such tactics burn out players fast.

More often, games offer gentler prods that prove more insidious despite appearing more forgiving. A game like King.com's immensely popular *Candy Crush Saga* offers an instructive example. The game is a match-three-style puzzle game, its core gameplay derived from PopCap's *Bejeweled*. Players match candies instead of gems, and each level requires the player to complete specific requirements—eliminating a particular number of a particular type of candy, reaching a score threshold, and so forth. The early levels are a cinch, but King.com carefully designs each level to become increasingly demanding. Failing a level results in the loss of a life, arcade-style, and losing all your lives ends the game. To continue, players can either wait a half hour for a new life to re-generate, pester a Facebook friend to play to receive a new life, or buy one as an impulse purchase. Players can also purchase special upgrades that assist in the completion of a level. The results are remarkable, from a business perspective. Pre-IPO disclosure reports suggested that King.com had been making between $500,000 and $850,000 *per day* from *Candy Crush*.[8] By early 2015, even after the title had begun to fall out of favor, it was estimated to be raking in closer to $1 million per day.[9]

While *FarmVille* and its ilk were often accused of barely re-sembling games, *Candy Crush* offers a mass-market return to the difficult, short-session play style of the coin-op arcade and the heyday of home consoles. But in so doing, it restructures the rela-tionship among the players, games, and developers. Some free-to-play advocates reason that trying a game for free and later choos-ing to pay a few dollars—or a few hundred—constitutes a similar transaction to making an outright purchase of a media product or series. And free-to-play publishers insist that most players re-ally do play for free—King.com told the *Guardian* that "70% of the people on the last level haven't paid anything."[10] Of course, that also means that most of Candy Crush's revenues come from a minority of players, a revenue pattern similar to casino gambling, which the economist Earl Grinols has demonstrated collects over half of all revenues from pathological gamblers.[11]

But as coin-op arcades, casino gaming, and mafioso racketeer-ing all demonstrate, a common *outcome* says very little about the nature of the *process* by which that outcome was reached. When one party pays $2 or $20 or $200 for a commodity sold by an-other and then both part ways, this relationship is different from one in which the seller offers access to a known, fixed experience for a per-use fee, or from one in which the seller offers a service for free that, if pursued in earnest, results in further financial, social, or time obligations. This seems like an obvious point—after all, earning a paycheck is different from winning a slot ma-chine jackpot or from shaking down a shopkeeper for protection money. And for that matter, spending that paycheck on food and rent is different from losing it on slot machines or ceding it to an extortionist.

Of course, game creators like Zynga and King.com aren't really the same as mafiosi. They're not committing racketeering in the legal sense. But likewise, they are also not the same as craftspeople selling their wares, buskers performing for handouts, or big publishers creating and distributing a singular media experience. The free-to-play structure isn't a "business model" tacked onto a game that might have been commercialized in any number of manners; it *creates* the game experience in relation to the commercial exigency of soliciting additional attention, word of mouth, and remuneration.

Yet, somehow, the games industry has convinced itself that the free-to-play distribution method is futuristic and desirable—"disrupting" the status quo of legacy media with its free downloads and in-app payments. Perhaps, but even if so, we must also admit that free-to-play refashioned the cultural role of videogames, a medium that spent so long struggling to overcome accusations of being mere children's toys and then vicious murder simulators. In response to these already awful cultural reference points, free-to-play realigns games with equally terrible influences: the duplicitous practices of casino operators and gangsters.

And this time around, perhaps the comparison is apt: the operators of these games do sometimes look more like racketeers than like entertainers. When Zynga finally went public in late 2011, it failed to exhibit the rocket ship liftoff the street had come to expect from hot tech company IPOs. Its shares rose from their $10 initial offering price to an all-time high of $14.69 in March 2012 before falling hard. During 2013 and 2014, the stock languished between $2 and $5 per share. The company shuttered studios and laid off workers in an attempt to stanch the bleeding, but performance didn't matter much for its early investors, directors, and executives, who had taken advantage of secondary-market sales and new venture investment to cash out part of their equity positions long before the company had to disclose its financials to the SEC and the public. Even after the IPO, Zynga insiders sold off hundreds of millions of dollars in a secondary offering unavailable to its employees, many of whom had been granted options and stock grants incentives as part of Silicon Valley standard operating procedure. Required SEC disclosures reveal that CEO Pincus cleared $200 million alone through this secondary offering.[12]

Somehow, despite Zynga's fall from grace, the dream of free-to-play still tempts game creators and players. Like most gamblers, players believe they are exceptions who will resist being duped into spending money on in-game items or energy, or who rationalize small payments as a reasonable concession after having been backed in a corner. Among game developers, the rank and file—always wary of ever-impending layoffs in an industry as fickle as it is fashionable—have resigned themselves to free-to-play as the new normal, or the will of the market. And executives, drunk at the prospect of quick cash-outs, have largely embraced the trend wholesale.

Perhaps that's because swindling has become the commonest and even the most respected practice in business and culture. Games publishers have come to believe that they *deserve* the more predictable, generous revenues that free-to-play games offer— finally, a salve from the burden of a hits-based industry like entertainment, they reason. Yet even the street has noticed that free-to-play looks like just as risky an investment as filmmaking or publishing absent diversification. In 2014 King.com completed a $5 billion IPO, making assurances along the way that it wouldn't fall into the same chasm Zynga did after going public, mostly by virtue of not being Zynga (the IPO was a disappointment, and nine months later the stock had fallen 60 percent below its IPO price). In advance of its offering, King.com had taken advantage of new, confidential IPO filings that allow it to hide business data it would have previously had to disclose, the same sorts of off-the-books dealings that allows tech darling insiders to operate surreptitiously before regulators notice. Like Wall Street, Silicon Valley is already a kind of mafia.

One need not convict game publishers of racketeering to be

justified in calling free-to-play games a racket. They create a surge of interest by virtue of their easy access, followed by a tidal wave of improbable revenue the games coerce out of players on terms that weren't disclosed at the outset. It's this lack of disclosure that makes free-to-play feel crooked: the game knows more than you about the stakes it presents, and it presents them given incomplete or withheld information while creating reasons for you to continue pursuing it. Just as the racketeer seeks to engender continued patronage through the threat of future disaster, so the free-to-play game seeks to extract continued attention through the promise of future accomplishment. Then its creators use that attention to build collective value that they cash in before anyone can see inside the machine that produced it. Like free Internet services more broadly, today business's real purpose is not to provide search or social or entertainment features but to create rapidly accelerating value as quickly as possible so as to convert that aggregated value into wealth.

Regardless, perhaps there's something to be gained from the free-to-play trend. Games are powerful and important partly because they help us test out the limits of ordinary life. This is why animals play, and why children play, but it's also why adults play. Under the best circumstances, a casino gambler understands the context of slot and table gaming as a way to tempt fate and luck, to put something at risk and to enjoy the sensation of that risk. And at their best, free-to-play games might offer a similar pleasure— the opportunity to see the economics of creators hoping to cash in on the speculative value of a massive player base via revenue extracted from its most addled participants. To feel the edges of the unholy reality of our current winner-take-all neo-gilded age. In light of this situation, perhaps we even *need* these free-to-play games, to help us see and understand the socioeconomic structure of the early twenty-first century. But, then again, if we do need them, it's only because the Silicon Valley technology industry has thrust such a profane era upon us, such that we would need to come to terms with its texture through play in the first place.

7

The Haute Couture of Videogames

Form, not function, makes *Hundreds* a status symbol

Some media exist for you to read, watch, play, or otherwise "consume," to use a common term for it. To devour it, to internalize it. Even though a book or a television show or a videogame isn't destroyed by this encounter like a cheesesteak or a firework might be, the creative work exists to be used up, to be made a part of ourselves. To inspire, to disturb, to persuade—whatever, really, so long as it enters and transforms us in some way.

But other media don't aspire to become incorporated. Instead, they are content skating along the surfaces of our lives rather than penetrating them. Fashion is like this: handbags, shoes, jackets, and all the rest literally cover our surfaces rather than our centers. Our clothes, our hair, our cars project appearances outward, even if we can be aware of and take satisfaction in the effect of those effects. So is most modern fine arts—most sculpture and painting, for example. Since Marcel Duchamp, the gallery and the museum have increasingly become places to be, much like certain clubs or restaurants become places to be seen. And some media work on the surface and when incorporated. Carrying a copy of the latest Mark Z. Danielewski tome has for one crowd much the same effect as wearing Prada shoes for another, but it can also be read for its content in addition to shelved for its cultural cachet.

One simple name for the surfaces of media is *design.* Despite the legacy of the Bauhaus in today's Apple electronics and their

< 56 >

knock-offs, and even despite the oppressive functionalism of fields like interaction design, design is what we *don't* use, what doesn't get transferred from an object to its reader, viewer, player, user, et cetera.

This is also why design is where things become *cool*. Cool isn't what something is *about,* but just what it *is.* Cool is like ether rather than alcohol. Trends may change its density, but when something is cool, it doesn't have to work for it. It just is, all at once, no waiting.

Like all cool things, *Hundreds* is a game that makes you cool by being near it. By having downloaded it, by touching it on your iPhone or iPad. *Hundreds* is a game for men with blond stubble and square chins and herringbone trousers. It's a game for women with perfect skin and long, thin fingers.

If that's not you, *Hundreds* is for you, too, in the same way the lobby bars of boutique hotels peppered with Ludwig Mies van der Rohe leather lounge chairs are for you. Part of what makes them cool is having you in them so the cool can attach to something, so the design can be perceived.

Hundreds is a physics-based puzzle game created by Adam Saltsman and Greg Wohlwend. Both have made popular web and iOS titles before, including early entries in the now-ubiquitous "jump and run" genre, *Canabalt* and *Solipskier.* Wohlwend has a penchant for baroque genre mash-ups like *Gasketball* (H.O.R.S.E meets *The Incredible Machine*) and *Puzzlejuice* (*Tetris* meets Boggle). Meanwhile, after the release of *Canabalt* in 2009, Saltsman experimented with sponsored projects, including the refreshingly modest film tie-in *The Hunger Games: Girl on Fire* and the surreal Old Spice deodorant advergame *Dikembe Mutombo's 4 1/2 Weeks to Save the World.* While their previous, individual work is dorky and wacky and charming and fun, *Hundreds* is *cool.* This is a more complex and bittersweet accomplishment than it seems.

The game is simple enough to understand. Black and gray circles appear on a white iPhone or iPad screen. Touching one or more of them causes them to grow, measured in units displayed within the circles. While any circle is touched and inflating, it must not make contact with another circle, or the game ends. To complete a puzzle, the total for all circles must reach one hundred (thus the game's title). There are one hundred levels, which grow more and more challenging as the game proceeds, each applying different physical motion to a set of circles and thus producing different challenges. As the levels progress, new types of circles emerge: bubbles that get in the way but can be popped, movable bumpers, spinning gears that deflate circles they contact, ice discs that freeze circles they touch, and so forth. Over time, things get quite dire: circles shrink instead of retaining their size, growth totals stop being displayed, circles become totally invisible unless contact is made with the screen, and so forth.

It doesn't sound like much. Another physics puzzler, a distraction good for wasting time in the waiting room or on a conference call. But unlike *Angry Birds* or *Cut the Rope*, *Hundreds* can't really be played casually. It requires full attention, two hands, and probably a table or a lap.

In part, this is because many of *Hundreds'* puzzles recommend or even require multitouch interaction for completion. Surprisingly, this is an uncommon feature of iOS titles, despite the fact that the device itself built its reputation on multitouch actions and gestures. *Fruit Ninja* may seem like it's best played with more than one finger, but it doesn't really much matter; just scrub madly with an index finger and avoid the bombs. By contrast, some of *Hundreds* levels feel like real more than virtualized physics puzzles. Take level eighty-nine, for example, which scatters five stationary, shrinking circles on the screen. Completing this puzzle not only required carefully balancing my iPad on my lap while applying pressure with multiple fingers on both hands but somehow doing so in coordination with my son, whom I had to recruit as an assistant.

For this reason, it's not accurate to call *Hundreds* a "casual game." It demands deep attention and almost perverse devotion to play well, let alone to complete (I'll admit, I still have yet to best level 100). Luckily, completion isn't really the point. It may not even be desirable.

Saltsman and Wohlwend market *Hundreds* as "a puzzle game about space, the space between you and the serene." But as with most puzzle games, there's nothing serene about playing *Hundreds*. It's maddening, infuriating, punctuated by small moments of pride that are quickly deflated upon realizing that they only lead to yet another screen filled with gray circles.

If there is serenity to be found in *Hundreds,* it lives less in the game's depths than in its surface, in its design. I don't mean its game design (the way that its elements behave and respond), nor do I mean its visual design (the simple geometry and colors that form its appearance), nor do I mean its interaction design (the use of one type of touch as a way to play). It's true that all three embody an elegant minimalism reminiscent of the Bauhaus design philosophy that Apple itself has popularized for contemporary computing culture. Those flavors of design are too ordinary and too antiseptic to capture the game's manner.

Rather, I mean the status of the entire game as a whole, as a complete surface over and above its parts. As a design object, *Hundreds* operates far more like Prada than like *Angry Birds*.

Like all cool things, *Hundreds* isn't really that compelling for what it attempts to deliver, for the "content" of its puzzles, whatever that might mean. Most designed objects have the luxury of not being able to try. Ray Ban Wayfarers and art deco leather club chairs don't have any meaning to relay in the first place, save the history of their own use. Even the iPhone doesn't really "mean" anything other than the fact of its existence, even if it can display and distribute media that can be consumed. The iPhone is about having an iPhone, about holding it and touching it and putting it down on the table nonchalantly.

With *Hundreds,* the iPhone or iPad gains a proverbial pair of sunglasses. It was the first game that allowed an iDevice to function actively rather than passively as the design object we so often celebrate. *Hundreds* is perhaps the only game you might look good playing perched on the leather hassock of a chichi bar that advertises mixologists instead of bartenders, you expanding circles while waiting for your friend or your date or even after he or she arrives, for that matter.

In fact, *Hundreds* sometimes feels more like a lobby bar than it does like a videogame. The game's music was created by Loscil, a Canadian artist whose electronic ambient sound often sets the chill mood popular in today's chichi lounges. Sitting there in your designer jeans, *Hundreds* is an accessory more like a martini than it is like a magazine. It's a videogame that you can imagine James Bond playing.

In fact, unlike most games, *Hundreds* will make you want to be cooler in order to do its presence justice. As the levels wear on, progress on the iPhone becomes difficult, like Finger Twister. By level seventy or so, switching to your iPad might make things easier (you do have an iPad, don't you?). But then again, the iPad is a bit bulky to cart around, particularly in public. Given that *Hundreds* is a game you might like to be *seen* playing, not just one you might resort to playing alone at the bus stop, perhaps it's better to update to an iPad Mini instead. Large enough to facilitate better play, but small enough to slip into the pocket of your Dolce & Gabbana jacket. A device you can clutch casually in one hand while fingering the stem of a cocktail glass in the other.

Design is no stranger to the tension between form and function. The Bauhaus style that inspired the legendary Braun designer Dieter Rams and shaped Apple's industrial design sensibility under Jony Ive purports to privilege function, removing anything unnecessary to the operation of a lamp, radio, or mobile phone. But eventually, form following function became its own form. The Marcel Breuer Wassily chair (or, later, the Herman Miller Aeron) may promise ergonomic efficiency, but really we love them for their surfaces, for their design. The same is true of the iPhone, whose one-button minimalist interface hardly makes the most functional phone. But who cares when it feels so good to hold, to touch, and to display?

I'm not sure even Saltsman and Wohlwend have grasped the implications of their creation, despite knowing full well that the game exudes more design than it does game design. Even still, the game's website seems to mistake the game for a *Bejeweled*-style Zen time waster. "You have millions of things on your mind," the site reads, surrounded by the game's circles, filled with icons representing life's demands. "Just take it 100 at a time," it continues as the user scrolls down the page, through trailers and accolades before concluding, "Let Hundreds unwind your mind."

But this is like mistaking Hermès for Land's End, or Philippe Starck for Cuisinart. *Hundreds* is not a time waster for the unwashed masses, not a refreshing distraction to quell the boredom or stress of bills or veterinary visits. It's a design object for players with crisp skirt pleats swishing over concrete floors, not sweatpants scuffling across supermarket tiles. It is not a game that distracts from boredom because players of *Hundreds* are above ennui, just like Aeron-cradled authors are above writer's block. The iPhone might be a device one can use on the toilet, but *Hundreds* certainly isn't a game one would play there. Do players of *Hundreds* even need to use the toilet? Probably not.

Some games get used up because we grow bored with them. Others can be finished, "won," completed. *Hundreds* may seem like a candidate for both boredom and resolution, but really it's neither, so long as you use it right.

The best sign of *Hundreds'* formal excess, the surest clue that it is a design object and not a consumable media object, is the remainder left within it. Upon completion of every tenth level or so, the game unlocks a cipher, a secret message encoded in letters or in symbols. Each one uses a different type of encryption, and when decoded they collectively unlock a special power that can be activated within the game.

A web search will reveal that, yes, there are some players

who have gone to the trouble of decoding each cipher encryption method and then decoding each cipher itself, through an
awkward and laborious data-entry interface custom-built for the
game. But no true player of *Hundreds* would bother. This busy-
work is beneath us. Yet, without it, there would be nothing to
disdain, no dumb misuse by the rabble who can't understand the
true nature of authentic design. The ciphers are the silly cocktail
special one forgoes on the spirits menu, the embossing detail that
distinguishes this year's handbags from last season's. For despite
its claims to inclusiveness, modern design works best when it's
exclusionary, when it's pretentious, when it speaks without saying
anything but just by *being there.*

8

Can the Other Come Out and Play?

Most games bring us together for collaboration or competition . . . but some do so for alienation

Players of the independent designer Jason Rohrer's early and widely praised art games *Passage* and *Gravitation* might have squinted when first trying his follow-up title, *Between*. Sure, they would recognize Rohrer's characteristic style: a preference for pixellation and visual austerity, the simple control over an abstract character, and an environment both naturalistic and human-made. But unlike many of his earlier games, *Between* does not directly model a human emotion or experience in the way *Passage* did with mortality or *Gravitation* with inspiration. At least, not at first blush.

Between is a two-player game, in the way that *PONG* is: it cannot be played by a single player. Once connected to a counterpart over the network, players still do not see each other's progress, at least not right away. Players are given little explicit direction beyond what objects on the screen imply: a tower of spaces for colored blocks stands at right, a wooden frame for placing blocks at center. The player can place and move blocks of a few different kinds and then "wake" or "sleep" to move between three similar versions of the game world. Four blocks placed in the wooden frame construct a new block that combines their components when the player wakes, and this process of constructing new blocks quickly becomes necessary to build up the tower.

< 63 >

The thing is, the player can place only primary additive mixable colored blocks to start (red, green, blue), but many of the blocks on the tower require secondary colors derived from additive mixes (cyan, magenta, yellow) as components. After a while, combinations of the latter set of color blocks appear based on mixes fashioned in the other player's tower.

The game gets hard very quickly. Part of the difficulty is a spatial relations challenge: as the tower gets bigger, the blocks require more complex components, which in turn have to be created through multiple sleep/wake cycles across the three renditions of the world. But the real trial comes from the player's lack of control over available resources: the cyan, magenta, and yellow-mixed blocks needed to make parts of the tower have to be coerced out of the other player somehow. The means for doing this is deliberately left out of the game. One option is for players to talk to each other and try to tease out the logic by which magic blocks appear. Another is for players to exercise patience and simply wait for the right blocks, an event that may never come to pass. Still another is to try to manipulate the second player's blocks indirectly by attempting to create blocks on the other player's screen that, when used, might result in needed resources on one's own. Two people playing on laptops in the same room enjoy an additional clue: as the tower builds up correctly, music begins to play with increasing detail and volume, which provides a hint about a counterpart's progress (in a brief statement accompanying the game, Rohrer discourages players from looking at each other's screens).

An ongoing debate rages about which is "better": single-player or multiplayer games. The game designer Raph Koster argues that single-player games are a "historical aberration" wrought by unconnected computers.[1] People, the argument goes, have played games together since the dawn of history as a way to test roles and enact traditions. Theorists of play like Johan Huizinga and Brian Sutton-Smith have made similar observations, studying the ways that play is central to human culture rather than set apart from it.[2] Critics, players, and the general public alike have observed how popular multiplayer or multiuser experiences, from *World of Warcraft* to *Facebook*, both improve and change the way we relate to other people. Indeed, one of the tired aphorisms of today's technology business culture is the promise to help people "connect with your friends."

Most videogames take one of a few tacks regarding play with others. Some games are solitary, with multiplayer experience limited to spectatorship *(Bioshock)* or hot-seat-style sequential play *(Asteroids)*. Others focus on competition, whether through strategy *(Diplomacy)* or combat *(Super Smash Bros.)*, synchrony *(CounterStrike)* or asynchrony *(Words with Friends)*. Still others focus on collaboration *(Little Big Planet)* or co-creation *(Minecraft)*. Social networking and massively multiplayer games might suggest a fourth kind of experience, that of socialization. And many games include variants or modes that cover solitary, competitive, and collaborative play.

But there are many more ways to understand how people relate to each other than just through solitude, competition, collaboration, or socialization. *Between* is such a game.

The concept of the "other" has a long and complex history in philosophy. Building on the thinking of Sigmund Freud and G. W. F. Hegel, the psychoanalyst Jacques Lacan advanced the idea of the other as a key organizing principle of the self. For the philosopher Emmanuel Levinas, the other remains forever unknowable and thus becomes the fundamental grounding for ethics. These thinkers understand others in a radical way: the other is not just "someone else" but something infinitely different, so much so that the chasm between self and other can never be traversed, mended, or united. From this frustration comes the concept's power. Unlike collaboration or competition or indeed solitude, the concept of the other reminds us that individual existence is composed partly from disconnectedness.

It is here that Rohrer's game takes root. Its title, *Between*, already suggests that the game deals with the space separating the two players more than the common goal that appears to unite them (constructing a tower of blocks). When the game begins, the player has the initial impression that the second player is unimportant; no trace of the other character appears on screen. As one completes the lower-level blocks, this sensation continues, until the reality of the blocks with secondary colors presents itself. Here, temporarily, the player feels as though a collaboration with the second player will be both fruitful and facile: all that is needed are enough secondary color blocks to allow the solitary construction of the tower. But then, and quickly, disappointment sets in: one player cannot simply request specific blocks from the other; rather, a complex and unseen process generates shadow blocks based on the structure the other player builds. This structure, too, remains unseen.

Here, a rendition of human experience through seemingly simple game dynamics takes root. Both players will likely wonder, perhaps aloud, what kind of game would make progress so inscrutable. The two may even try to strategize, carefully sharing moves in an attempt to trace the edges of the computational process used to generate counterpart blocks on the other player's screen. But this process, too, has its limits: eventually compound blocks must be created across multiple screens in the game, increasing the cognitive load of both players to the breaking point.

Between does not try to create identification through collaboration. The game aims to create a relationship between two players that focuses both on the chasm that separates them as human beings, rather than on a common foe, or each other as foes, or as a medium for social interaction.

When we talk about games, we normally use the language of conjunction, whether through accompaniment ("to play with") or conflict ("to play against"). Whether for competition, collaboration, or socialization, multiplayer games aim to connect people in the act of play itself. *Between* takes on a very different charge: it aims to remind players of the abyss that forever separates them from another. In the face of this gulch, the best we can do is to attempt to trace the edges of our cohort's gestures and signals, as players of *Between* do when they interpret the origins of the weird, mottled colored patterns that appear as if from nowhere on their screens.

If most multiplayer games are conjunctive, *Between* is disjunctive. It is a game that aims to disturb notions of cohesion rather than to create them. And if any common sympathy arises from the experience, it is a feeling of comfort in the commonality of one's inevitable isolation. Herein lies the strange logic of otherness: apart from death, it is the one thing we human beings all share. And in so doing, it joins us even as it pushes us apart.

When *Between* was released in 2008—before today's independent games scene had really arrived, but after it was clear what it meant to make games independently, as a solo artist—it experienced a rare moment of proxy success. The game won the Innovation Award in the 2009 Independent Games Festival, and some had the (probably reasonable) impression that the award was meant to acknowledge Rohrer's earlier work rather than the somewhat confusing game that was actually nominated. Particularly since the game was flawed in a potentially fatal way: without any signal that an other is present and that the work the other is working on takes place in relation to you as self, the game risks obscuring the experience it hopes to create.

Two years later, Coco & Co's similar game *Way* attempted to overcome these defects. Created in part by Chris Bell, who had been a part of the team that created *flOw, Flower,* and *Journey* at thatgamecompany, the game embraces some of the same concepts of shared experience that later appeared in the last of those games. *Journey* makes no particular demand that players who appear in each other's game necessarily need to work together. By contrast, *Way* demanded collaboration in the same way that *Between* had done. But where Rohrer had hidden all clues about the operation of that collaboration, demanding that players figure it out on their own, *Way* clearly explains what its players must do to progress.

In the game, players find a familiar two-dimensional plat-forming environment. The usual navigating, jumping, and lever-actuation routine allows each player to traverse the environment. But soon enough, progress becomes impossible; the player can see what has to be done but can no longer make progress to ac-complish it. At this stage, the game reveals that not one but two players are needed to complete the game's puzzles. As in *Journey,* these matches are made automatically and invisibly. *Between* had asked players to explicitly create a game together, but *Way* and *Journey* rely on anonymity as a fundamental part of relating to the player-as-other.

Way becomes a game about attempting to communicate with a stranger absent ordinary language. Players can instruct their characters to gesture toward targets, levers, or platforms by point-ing a hand in their direction on a split-screen, and they can ac-tivate abstract grunts to create auditory signals. If *Between* was a game about the logic of otherness, *Way* becomes its emotional counterpart—and a rehearsal for the different, higher-fidelity version of emotional companionship that Bell would help real-ize in *Journey.* But even as *Way* succeeds in embracing a collab-orative gameplay stripped of communication, it also assumes another, different kind of communication: that of ostension and interjection, which are themselves culturally specific modes of communication.

On the one hand, the game improves *Between*'s model of dis-junctive multiplayer experience by better clarifying a goal and a way to accomplish it. On the other hand, *Way* proves that any at-tempt to clarify otherness always returns it to familiarity. Perhaps any attempt to represent otherness always destroys it by making familiarity possible. *Between* fights against this trap by making almost everything about the game incomprehensible—to the point that many players will find it simply unplayable. Such is the gentle dance of comprehending alienation. The moment one finds recognition, the idea of the other becomes subsumed into the domain of the same, of the self. But without that recognition, any particular other remains indistinguishable from the nebulous universe.

Before you conclude that the disjunctive multiplayer experience of *Between* or *Way* is limited to the domain of weird independent art games, consider another, very different title that also employs disjunctive multiplay: *Spore.*

When Will Wright first began talking publicly about his "SimEverything" title, one way he described it was as a "massively single player game." The game's many editors would allow players to create their own creatures, vehicles, buildings, and even planets. To construct a rich, credible universe, these objects would be uploaded silently to a server, where they would then be deployed into other players' games.

Unlike purely generative stuffs, some semblance of coherence would be ensured, since human hands would have created each object to be shared. But unlike so many popular user-generated content websites, *Spore*'s various matter would not promote individual creativity as its first goal. Rather, it would serve as the other in *Spore*'s vast galaxy. The creatures, vehicles, and buildings that the game draws from a common pool become the beings, conveyances, and shelters of alien species. As in *Between*, *Spore*'s players do not work together or against one another. Instead, each player's creations, so familiar and transparent to the individual player, become the aliens in other players' games. But as in *Way*, players of *Spore* have some sense of where these other aliens came from and the process by which they arose, thus orienting them toward the idea of that alienation. *Alien*, a word that literally means "other," evokes anxiety because it suggests something utterly unfamiliar, making the alien creatures of *Spore* an effective source of disjunctive play.

In today's world, everywhere we turn we are enjoined toward commonality. Facebook wants us to see the same groups our friends join, the same ads others like us click. Amazon and Netflix help us understand what others who liked what we like also bought or borrowed, and YouTube and Instagram help us see what graced the retinas of others who watched or looked at what we just encountered. In the face of such obsession with commonality, disjunctive multiplayer experiences remind us that no matter how similar cultures, marketplaces, or communities might make us, some aspects of other people remain ever out of reach.

9

A Way of Looking

The moving photograph of *Mirror's Edge*

When we use a toaster, or a sweater, or a word-processing software package, we have certain functional expectations. A toaster
should brown bread evenly and consistently. A sweater should
keep a body warm without fraying or stretching out from repeated
use. A word processor should help automate the crafting of docu-
ments without requiring specialized expertise.

Some of our expectations of such objects are cosmetic. We like
our toasters to match the decor in our kitchens, our sweaters to
be woven with the colors and styles of the current season. But the
history of software as a tool for work has made most cosmetic
demands for software relate to matters of usability: buttons and
menus should be in convenient locations, actions should feel
consistent and predictable, conventions set by previous iterations
of a software package should be respected, even if lightly refined.

In the field of human–computer interaction (HCI), these values of software design are sometimes grouped under the term
transparency. A good software tool, like a good toaster, is supposed to show us exactly how it should be used and then meet our
expectations as users immediately and consistently.

The media theorists Jay Bolter and Diane Gromala suggest a
different way to look at software, especially software that seeks to
explore ideas rather than to serve as tools.[1] Bolter and Gromala
point out that the concept of transparency casts software as a
window—a clear surface that seeks to disappear as it reveals

< 71 >

a functional affordance. This conception works well for tools but poorly for art. Instead, the two suggest another metaphor, a mirror. Unlike a window, a mirror's job is to reflect back on its users, to give them a new perspective on themselves and their place in the world.

Videogames are software, but they are not meant to serve the same function as spreadsheets. They are not tools that provide a specific and solitary end but experiences that spark ideas and proffer sensations. Sure, videogames have interfaces, like toasters have browning levers, like sweaters have cuffs, like word processors have font menus. But too often we mistake the demands of these interfaces (and the in-game actions they facilitate) with the actions of tools. We gripe when a game doesn't do what we expect, rather than ask what such an unexpected demand means in the context of the game.

The phenomenon can be found in most game reviews: beefs about controls, graphical style, fictional direction. One title to suffer the wrath of critics desperate to find a window out of their console also carries the opposite strategy in its very title: *Mirror's Edge,* a game about a rooftop messenger in a surveillance state dystopia.

Some found the game constricting and overly linear, concluding that it did not deliver what it promised.[2] Others defended the title on the grounds of experimentalism.[3] When a filmmaker tries to do something new, argues Keith Stuart in the *Guardian,* we appreciate innovation for its own sake. Still others attempted to rationalize the game's perceived defects as design lessons. Channeling a designer's input, the critic Leigh Alexander suggests that poor level design caused some of the game's frustrating repetition.[4] Eventually she concluded that it just wasn't executed well.[5]

These are all reasonable sentiments about a piece of media. One role of the critic is to point out flaws in a work (here's one: why does a game about rooftop messengers involve no actual messengering?). But none of these reactions are satisfactory ways to respond to the game *exclusively.* Asking that a game does exactly what its player expects risks eliminating the possibility that it might offer a new way to understand the world. Supporting design novelty risks fetishizing innovation for its own sake over the ways that such innovation helps construct meaningful experiences. And focusing on design lessons risks turning each example of our medium into an instrumental postmortem-in-miniature, a tragic progression toward inaccessible perfection, one that fails to allow any single example to speak on its own terms.

But perhaps all these concerns miss the fact that *Mirror's Edge* is an immensely successful interactive mirror, in Bolter and Gromala's sense of the word.

The photographer Garry Winogrand famously said that he took pictures to see what things look like photographed. This apparent tautology is actually a brilliant insight into that medium: the practice of taking and looking at photographs is one of defamiliarizing the ordinary to make it strange, sublime, disturbing, or otherwise revealing. Photography re-presents the world not as it is but as it appears through the form of the photograph.

Mirror's Edge is a game about another way of looking. It asks the player to see a credible, familiar world filled with cars, machines, hallways, and buildings in a different light. Each surface becomes a potential affordance for movement, and the player must learn to see fences, forklifts, ledges, and subway cars as tools of locomotion rather than as objects of industry. The game's promising if slapdash dystopic fiction offers an entry into this practice, by persuading the player that the city is encumbered with a classic appearance versus reality problem. Visually, the game brings about this means of looking by literally whitewashing as much of the environment as possible, such that its surfaces reveal very little. The fact that nearly everything is white—including the plants— acts as a perceptual reset.

"Runner vision," the feature that colors "usable" objects in red, acts as a way to help the player overcome such an uncanny way to see a familiar world. It is tempting to see this feature as a cheat, a way to avoid asking the player to do something perceptually unreasonable. But once so much of the game's urban environment is stripped of pigment, the addition of new pigment delivers a way to see things. Like a photograph that highlights an unexpected object through selective focus, runner vision draws the eye to the detritus that would otherwise seem like visual noise, reattenuating it into signal. And because *Mirror's Edge* is a videogame instead of a photograph, it is able to extend a way of looking into a way of moving as well.

Parkour, or free running, serves as a primary inspiration for *Mirror's Edge*. The construction of another way of looking and moving offers the first way to adapt that activity: like the skateboarder, the free runner sees the world differently, as a set of affordances for previously unintended means of locomotion.

But there is something else about parkour that *Mirror's Edge* translates deftly: a sense of fluidity. The free runner does not simply see the city differently; he sees it as such without hesitation, moving immediately from step to wall to landing to ledge to ground. This sense of effortless continuity is what makes parkour beautiful to watch and, I presume, gratifying to experience. Not only must the successful free runner make divergent use of familiar surfaces, but also he must do so as smoothly as possible.

Mirror's Edge deploys two main strategies to create the experience of fluidity. The first is its first-person perspective, an unusual, risky decision that alienates some players, those unable to get over the fact that the Unreal 3 engine in which the game is built would have afforded a more straightforward third-person viewpoint. The game would indeed probably have been easier to play with the camera locked behind its main character, Faith. But the game's purpose was not to make movement predictable and easy—to make it transparent, in the lingo of HCI. Rather, *Mirror's Edge* attempts to create a sense of vertigo that the player must constantly overcome to reorient Faith toward her next objective. The rewards for success are remarkable: running to a sprint and properly vaulting a fence produces a sense of physical mastery commensurate with the parkour expert.

The second is its unusual level structure, one designed for difficulty. *Mirror's Edge* is a hard game; the number of times a player, even a good one, will fail is enormous. When such failures occur, the game often asks the player to restart from a particularly punitive location, demanding that he work back to a point where, inevitably, he is likely once again to tumble violently down to earth.

Unlike the *Assassin's Creed* series, which adapts the fluidity of parkour by making movement consistently easy, *Mirror's Edge* adapts that fluidity by making it hard. But what initially seems like a punitive design gaffe actually carries a crucial payload: requiring the player to reattempt sets of runs ensures that the final, successful one will be completed all in one go. This is not the same type of frustration that one finds in *Mega Man*: the punitive levels are not conduits for final accomplishment and trophy but for mastery over the very process of moving through the levels themselves.

Though it emphasizes running, jumping, ducking, and vaulting, *Mirror's Edge* also lives up to its first-person camera by offering gun-toting. While it's allegedly possible to finish the game without offing any hostiles, most players will find such an achievement hard to accomplish. But more importantly, trying to do so would mean missing out on one of the game's best features: its simulation of weakness.

Faith is not strong in combat. She is easily overcome by a few blows of a firearm stock or far fewer shots from its barrel. Her fragility in combat is no greater than her fragility in movement (death is easy in this game), but the player's sensation of Faith's weakness in the former helps accentuate her strength in the latter. Faith can run fast, jump accurately, slip in-between and under obstacles for shelter. She can bounce off walls with ease and balance on precarious outcroppings. But she can't really melee without becoming overpowered. And she can't wield a gun like a Delta Squad soldier.

The player's best strategy for combat is close-range fighting while in motion, either with jump-kicks launched from vaults off a higher surface, slides and shin-kicks that disable an opponent, or weapon takeaways that require precise timing. All these gestures are acts that Faith is good at performing; she is a runner, after all.

Then there are the firearms. Once Faith picks up a gun, her movement slows considerably. She becomes less agile, and certain acrobatics become unavailable. She can't easily withstand the kickback of larger guns, which require careful aiming. Yet stopping to sight an enemy is antithetical to the expressive mission of *Mirror's Edge*; it is a game about rapid, fluid, human movement, not standing still with a slab of dumb machinery.

Combat in *Mirror's Edge* is consequently miserable. Miss the right timing to grab a rifle and down you'll go. Lumbering through a gun battle feels brute force and ungratifying. It's not uncommon to enter a new area, see a hostile, and feel genuinely angry and disappointed at having to deal with him. The game is a shooter that makes you hate to shoot.

Instead of reading the game's combat system as a weakness, we can understand *Mirror's Edge* instead as a game about a character's weakness. Whereas so many games simulate unlimited power, *Mirror's Edge* shows us the limits of power—not only that of Faith, but that of the entire first-person shooter genre. Its lack of on-screen interfaces undermines the idea that "health" is a valid way to represent ability. Instead, *Mirror's Edge* replaces the pleasure of violent engagement with the pleasure of running away, footfalls tapping pavement gratifyingly as bullets zip by.

Mirror's Edge is not a perfect game, perhaps, but it is something more important: it is an interesting game. It can be played and experienced on its own terms, for its own sake, if players would only allow themselves to take a single videogame specimen at face value rather than as yet another datapoint on the endless trudge toward realistic perfection.

While Keith Stuart's rejoinder against meeting expectations does remind us that innovation offers an important avenue for creativity, to privilege experimentalism still implies a view toward titles of the future. We should stop looking at the games we make and play in terms of how closely the vistas they open match the ones in our mind when we come to them. Rather than see these works as mere toasters or word processors meant to deliver on our expectations while we await a better version to come along, we must begin to understand what games can offer us today: how they can serve as a mirror that presents a new view of our own experience of the world rather than as a window polished to an incrementally greater shine, facing that same green pasture of familiarity. With *Mirror's Edge,* we have one such example: a game about looking and moving in an unfamiliar way, about feeling frail when we are used to feeling powerful, and then feeling powerful again when we reject the convention to fight and choose instead to run like hell.

10

Free Speech Is Not a Marketing Plan

For players, creators, and even the U.S. Supreme Court, games are a protected form of speech. Will they ever have anything to say?

Imagine a videogame about the difficult life of a typical but troubled adolescent. He's the product of a broken home and alienated from his parents, who are more interested in the novelty of their new marriage than in the responsibility of raising a child. He's been in and out of different schools and finds it hard to make friends. Disappointing relationships make it hard for him to trust other kids, and more so other adults. He acts out and gets in trouble, sometimes from boredom, sometimes from belligerence, and sometimes just to get some attention, since he doesn't get any at home. If you ask him, he'd probably tell you that most people are not to be trusted, that they'd rather push you around than give you the time of day. Rather than wait to be proved right, he might knock you down first if you have the wrong look about you. He sees himself as an outsider and despises cliques, although he really has a lot in common with a number of mainstream social groups. He's had a few crushes but never had the chance to really pursue amorous relationships, partly because he never had a positive model for them at home and partly because he tends to get in trouble before he can make a move. He has intellectual promise but rarely lives up to his potential, mostly because he doesn't know how to channel his positive and negative energy into prosocial pursuits.

< 78 >

The videogame would allow the player to live in the shoes of this typical adolescent during a time-compressed academic calendar year, to understand the conflicted social situation for a troubled teen. The game might be appropriate for teenagers, especially as a curative. But it would really be targeted at adults, especially the parents, educators, and policymakers who have the power, authority, and life experience to help counsel teens like him in the real world.

This description sounds like it might have been lifted from a grant proposal for a serious game, one that a researcher might submit to the Department of Education, or the National Institutes of Health, or the National Science Foundation. But it's not. It's the premise for Rockstar Games controversial 2006 title *Bully*.

Of course, you'd never see a marketing slogan or a mainstream media article that puts the game in those terms. Instead, you see coverage of high-profile lawsuits that try to declare the game obscene. You see predictions that the game will impel kids to open fire on their classmates. You see reports of entire retail chains that refuse to sell it. You see calls for boycotts of the game from media watchdog groups. You see grievances over another perceived ratings board failure. You see calls for increased legislation of videogames and government control over the practices of their distribution and sale.

But you also see abstract defenses of the game in the name of free speech. Self-important, empty journalistic replies that report yet another case of an age gap between cultures. Repetitions of tired rejections of the effect of media on behavior. Vindictive defenses that pedantically address detractors' grievances in enumerated lists. Rationalistic defenses of menial violence in the name of kiddie-vigilante justice. Intellectualized comparisons to censorship and regulation arguments in every medium since the midcentury.

No matter how absurd the public response to *Bully* might seem to those deeply immersed in videogame culture, the game community's own responses are framed almost entirely within the language and issues of that public debate. Nowhere do game reviewers, players, journalists, or developers discuss the game's meaning on its own terms—neither in praise nor in riposte.

We can understand this state of affairs through the lens of "seriousness." On the one hand, the public detractors of *Bully* do take the game seriously, as a threat and a danger but not as a cultural artifact. The videogame community, on the other hand, did not take the game seriously at all. It allowed the legislators and attorneys and media watchdogs to define the terms of the debate.

As in the case of its more well-known *Grand Theft Auto* titles and the controversy that always surrounds them, Rockstar doesn't help matters, and not just because its releases seek out controversy to create a wake of free publicity. The company exacerbates the ambiguous meaning that surrounds the game by remaining silent about it. When Hollywood studios release films, even controversial ones, they launch huge press junkets to discuss them. They send the stars on *The Tonight Show* to talk about the film. They acknowledge that they take artistic license and make claims about the topics they choose to address.

Taking *Bully* seriously means acknowledging that the game has something to say about the world, not just that the world has something to say about it. It means assessing how effectively the game tackles the topic of bullying and how meaningful are its claims about it.

And in truth, those claims, nonexistent though they might have been, bear dubious fruit. The game certainly sets the stage convincingly. The player's character, Jimmy Hopkins, is dropped off at Bullworth Academy by his indifferent mother and stepfather, who are on their way to a lavish honeymoon. This introductory cut-scene doesn't provide a complete backstory for Jimmy, but it does suggest that his home life has been less than supportive. The implication is that his father was never around, and his mother is much more interested in her boy toys than in her son. Jimmy feigns disinterest, but also offers a telling one-liner: "Why did you have to marry him?" This context is important, because it gives the player a partial explanation for Jimmy's cynicism and aggressive tendencies. Clearly he's been neglected, and clearly he's tried to reach out to his family for attention and support, but there was none to be found.

The most powerful experience I had in the game came shortly after I was first given control of Jimmy. The introductory task asks the player to visit the headmaster in his office, which is located in a building just across the quad. The task is intended to orient the player to controls, maps, and other interface details, but it effectively summarizes the title's core experience. Students mill in the quad and buildings, either verbally and physically abusing each other or receding from verbal and physical attacks. Staying out of the way of the bullies (bullies in the game conveniently have their own clique, and all wear the same clothes) avoids tussles. If you stand in front of the wrong locker, expect to get shoved out of the way.

The experience was mildly harrowing, even though it was just a caricature of the particular social ills of high school. The game actually simulated social discomfort. I found myself thinking, "What did I do to deserve this from these kids?" The fact that *Bully* can succeed in producing this kind of response speaks to the power of the game, and the medium. *Bully* promises to make the player uncomfortable, to make him or her hate this virtual boarding school and to *want* to risk punishment to set things right.

The game's missions and emergent dynamics, however, don't cash out this promise. The player learns how to break into lockers, how to sweet talk girls to win favors, how to fight (fisticuffs, slingshots, stinkbombs, etc.). In typical Rockstar fashion, the game privileges the underdogs—nerds and girls—and the player spends most of his time undermining the bullies and the jocks in order to even the social pecking order. Despite the counter-media rhetoric, authority structures in the game are fairly weak by design, since even the adults in Jimmy's world can't be trusted. The player does have to attend classes or risk punishment for truancy, but the school subject mini-games are rudimentary and contingent (an anagram game for English, a rhythm matching game for chemistry, a *Qix* clone for art, etc.). Time is so heavily compressed in the game that attending class becomes a fairly minor part of the experience anyway. The same goes for truancy and getting caught by prefects. Yes, the player does endure reprimand, but the consequences are akin to arrest in *Grand Theft Auto*—lose some items, and some time. Waiting for the console to load the headmaster office cut-scenes feels like more punishment than losing a pocketful of stink bombs.

As with most of the Rockstar titles, the best social commentary in *Bully* is ambient. In *Grand Theft Auto,* it was the hilariously satirical radio shows. In *Bully,* it's the conversations among Bullworth students, which satirize the shallow nature of high school social roles.

Sweeping away all the dust that *Bully* left in the wake of its release, it's hard to defend the game, not because it might be a public nuisance or a danger to kids, but because it could have been so much more scathing a critique of high school social politics than it turned out to be. Jimmy defends the weak and undermines the school's tormentors, but the player never feels much empathy for any of them. Bullying is overly stylized, with verbal and physical attacks slung almost at random, a result of Rockstar's continued resistance to moving beyond the stock affordances of game engines' facility to simulate the physical world to model inner lives for characters beyond the ones hard-coded into the cut-scenes. Even Jimmy's relationships with girls are limited to wearing down their apathy with flowers or candy until they agree to kiss him.

Many so-called serious games—games created for educational, corporate, or governmental use—privilege pedantic learning theories and organizationally endorsed messages over earnest depictions of their subject. Rockstar's approach is the right one: model the broken dynamics of high school and give the player an embodied experience of negotiating those dynamics. But in this case, the spotty follow-through not only affects this specific representation of life among bullies but also risks poisoning the topic for those who might come to it later, differently. Bullying in videogames is marked terrain, at least for the time being.

When we combine the game's failings with Rockstar's characteristically silent apathy about its artistic intent, it's tempting to conclude that the game is little more than a provocation, a good idea with enough neutralizing rhetoric in its design to deflect the most obviously anticipated media criticisms. Of all the people who should take *Bully* more seriously than they have, perhaps the worst offender is Rockstar themselves.

Rockstar isn't alone. Four years after the release of *Bully*, and under the shadow of the U.S. Supreme Court's ruling that videogames are protected under the First Amendment, Electronic Arts caved to public pressure and removed the Taliban from its then forthcoming edition of *Medal of Honor.*

The game had been courting controversy for months. In a departure from its heritage as a game glorifying World War II–era combat, the 2010 edition of the long-running series took up the ongoing war in Afghanistan. Purportedly developed in consultation with U.S. Tier 1 Special Operations Forces, the game promises that players "will step into the boots of these warriors and apply their unique skill sets to a new enemy in the most unforgiving and hostile battlefield conditions of present day Afghanistan."[1]

As with *Bully,* it was a promising idea for a videogame. After all, warfare has changed considerably since the mid-twentieth century, and the game-playing public might benefit from an experience of modern warfare drawn from the pages of the news rather than the pages of fantasy novels.

Certainly other media have taken up this goal. The documentary film *Restrepo,* for example, chronicles a terrifying year of unforgiving impasse in Afghanistan's dangerous Korangal Valley, which is sometimes called "the deadliest place on earth" by American troops. Like Kathryn Bigelow's film *The Hurt Locker* and David Simon and Ed Burns's miniseries *Generation Kill,* *Restrepo* eschews geopolitical context in favor of the raw experience of modern war. In fact, that's really the film's main point:

despite home-front rhetoric about the political justifications for extended wars in Afghanistan and Iraq, the modern soldier's experience is neither rooted in nor justified by political accomplishment. In a strange and perversely poetic inversion, it is little more than an exercise in terror—for terrorist and for liberator alike.

For its efforts, *Restrepo* won the Grand Jury Prize for best documentary at the Sundance Film Festival. A small cultural victory, to be sure, but a poignant one, too, in light of the incredible pointlessness of the American occupation of the Korangal Valley. On April 14, 2010, the United States closed its outpost there, admitting that no military or political progress had been made during the four years it had been in operation.

Restrepo is hardly the most controversial of recent art about a contemporary political issue. It's tame, in fact, compared with the long history of filmic button-pushing. Movies have mostly stirred controversy through depictions of sex and perversion (a subject about which videogames haven't gotten to first base), but war has had its share of filmic contentiousness, too.

Michael Cimino's 1978 film *The Deer Hunter,* for example, won the Oscar for Best Picture despite stirring up considerable debate about the historical accuracy of its depiction of Vietcong atrocity. More recently, Michael Moore's 2004 documentary *Fahrenheit 9/11* earned public ire for its take on the Bush administration's handling of the war on terror. Among the latter film's controversies were accusations of commercial censorship, as Moore had accused Disney's Miramax division of refusing to distribute the film for fear of political retribution in the state of Florida, where Jeb Bush served as governor at the time. (As it happens, Disney sold Miramax in 2010, for $100 million less than it spent to buy free-to-play social gaming studio Playdom the very same month.)[2]

Despite ruffling feathers, these two films serve as relatively modest specimens of art made to spur public debate in the ways that the First Amendment is supposed to facilitate. They represent resolve and intention on the part of their creators, who hoped to advance potentially unpopular positions as a matter of speech, not just as a matter of marketing. And as works made for private gain, they advocate for the amalgamation of public and commercial speech, for they draw the public interest out of the accident of industrial production and distribution.

How does Electronic Arts measure up? In creating a videogame about the war in Afghanistan, the company had at first stood firm against myriad accusations of the tastelessness of allowing players to take on the roles of enemy operatives in the game, particularly the Taliban. UK defense secretary Liam Fox had decried the game as offensive and shocking, noting that British families had lost fathers at the hands of the Taliban.[3] On Fox News, Karen Meredith, the mother of a fallen American soldier, had called the game "disrespectful" for "turning war into a game."[4] And the retailer GameStop declared its intention not to sell the game on military bases "out of respect for our past and present men and women in uniform."[5] EA spokespeople smartly countered that opposition is a part of conflict and that videogames offer a unique opportunity for citizens to play both sides, presumably to understand the differences in motivation or experience on either side of the conflict.

Such controversy continued, with its related publicity benefits, even despite a lack of information about just what it would *mean* to play the Taliban in *Medal of Honor.* As *Restrepo* showed, the pure anguish of the Afghan war may obliterate the very notion of "good guys" and "bad guys" in Afghanistan in the first place. A generous interpreter might hope for such a subtle reveal in the game, one that might send a knowing chill down the spines of its presumably sophisticated playership. But EA's final move in the *Medal of Honor* saga seems instead to reveal that its interest in Afghanistan and the Taliban in particular never had anything whatsoever to do with a position on foreign war—or really on anything whatsoever.

In a statement issued October 1, 2010, *Medal of Honor* executive producer Greg Goodrich caved to "concern over the inclusion of the Taliban in the multiplayer portion of our game."[6] Goodrich clarified that the opposition wouldn't be removed from the title but would instead simply be "renamed from Taliban to Opposing

Force." His statement concluded with a note of appreciation for troops serving overseas, clear contrition for the studio's perceived indignities. Crucially, Goodrich entreated the public to note the following: "This change should not directly affect gamers, as it does not fundamentally alter the gameplay." This one statement should cause considerable distress, as it suggests a troubling conclusion about *Medal of Honor* as a work of public speech.

To wit: it implies that the Taliban never had any meaningful representation in the game anyway. If a historically, culturally, and geographically specific enemy can simply be recast in the generic cloth of "opposition," then why was it was called "Taliban" in the first place? And if the Afghan war in which this *Medal of Honor* is set was one explicitly meant to drive the Taliban from their strongholds in Afghanistan, why should it matter that the game is set in that nation in the present day at all? In short, how was this *Medal of Honor* title meant to be a game about this war in particular?

If the presence or absence of the Taliban "does not fundamentally alter the gameplay," then perhaps it did not matter that this particular Islamist terrorist group found its way into the game in the first place. And since EA has not altered the experience but only renamed the enemy, then whatever simulation of Taliban life *Medal of Honor* does offer remains the same save the letters by which it is annotated on-screen. If a meaningful simulation of the Taliban ever existed, one that meant more than "the name for the current enemy that is in Afghanistan," then the studio would have had to admit that *no other name* can be given for that opposing force and that to hedge would ruin the unique artistic expression the game hoped to communicate.

EA's statement is one of *commercial* political convenience, precisely the sort of hedge that undermines free speech protections by distancing them from earnest contributions to public ideas. Says Goodrich, "We are making this change for the men and women serving in the military and for the families of those who have paid the ultimate sacrifice—this franchise will never willfully disrespect, intentionally or otherwise, your memory and service." As it turns out, government pressure may have contributed to the about-face. According to a report published soon after Goodrich's statement, the U.S. Army may have threatened to withdraw its support for the game had the playable Taliban remained.[7]

Whether such duress ever materialized is irrelevant, especially if Goodrich and his team don't really have anything to communicate about Afghanistan in the first place. *Restrepo* and *The Hurt Locker* also de-emphasize geopolitics in favor of the experience of soldiering, but neither set of filmmakers would ever have argued that their respective settings and contexts were irrelevant to that experience. Yet in an interview with a game industry trade publication, *Gamasutra,* Goodrich makes this claim quite clearly, declaring that he intended the game to be "devoid of politics or political discussion or debate." Goodrich further clarified, "I think we've always approached [the game] in the sense that it's not about the war itself. We've not approached as a game about Afghanistan, or a game about Al Qaeda. This is not a game about the Taliban. This is not a game about local tribal militias or warlords."[8] Instead, Goodrich suggests that the game is about "individuals doing their job," a kind of milquetoast soldier's homage: "Let's support them, let's get them home."

To review: Electronic Arts made a war game about the U.S.-led war against the Taliban in Afghanistan, but that game is not about war, not about Afghanistan, not about the Taliban, not political, and not interested in making or supporting any discussion.

Instead, *Medal of Honor* became another well-produced first-person shooter, one that invoked a recent war as a marketing gimmick to accompany an equally generic plea to "support our troops." Playing as the Taliban never mattered anyway. It was just a menu item, so no big deal to remove or rename it. Just a marketing tag on the box. Just a clever hook to spin free publicity, and just an inconvenient but essentially irrelevant feature to drop when the Army brass raised its eyebrows.

How to square this total unconcern with earnest speech

with another statement issued on October 1, 2010, from the Entertainment Software Association about the *Schwarzenegger v. Entertainment Merchants Association* Supreme Court case? The action was seen as a significant victory for the videogame industry in matters of free speech. In a brief filed with the court, the ESA argues that "video games are a popular form of modern artistic expression involving classic themes, storylines and player involvement, affording them the same First Amendment protections as other media, such as books and movies."

Yet as *Medal of Honor* and *Bully* demonstrate, wealthy corporations like Electronic Arts and Rockstar that fund the ESA to lobby on their behalf are typically not the ones to take up such a charge in earnest. In an inversion unseen in any other popular medium, almost all truly challenging artistic expression in games comes primarily from rogue creators, independents whose political and artistic ambitions typically *conflict with* rather than complement their connections with the commercial marketplace.

Will commercial videogames ever care enough about the world they share with war and sex and crime and brutality to want to speak about those issues in earnest, in public, despite the negative reactions or even *in order to elicit* those negative reactions? Or will they merely want to sell bits and plastic at $60 a go, any one just as good as the last so long as its review scores hold up?

Free speech is not a marketing plan. Free speech is only any good if videogame creators take advantage of its invitation. Eventually, perhaps, the mass market videogame developers will begin to speak like they mean it. Otherwise, they just make a mockery of those who do, those who have the courage to go out on a limb, to compromise their popularity, their success, their safety even on behalf of something more than a quarterly target or a bonus check. Free speech is defended in courts, but it is practiced on the streets and in the media by people who want to intervene in their world, not just to occupy it. Commercial videogames deserve a place at that table, to be sure. Whether they will ever choose to show up is an open question.

11

Shaking the Holocaust Train

Gestural control is better used for meaningful
player action than for input

Games have flaunted gestural interfaces for years now. The
Nintendo Wii and its copycats became the most familiar example in the late 2000s, but such interfaces can be traced back
decades: Sony's EyeToy; Bandai's Power Pad; Nintendo's Power
Glove; Amiga's Joyboard; the rideable cars and motorbikes of the
1980s arcade; indeed, even Nintendo's own progenitors of the Wii
Remote, like *Kirby Tilt 'n' Tumble* for GameBoy Color.

By 2010 all three major console manufacturers had released
gestural interfaces. Nintendo introduced the Wii Balance Board,
a device capable of detecting pressure and movement on the floor,
as well as the Wii MotionPlus, a Wii Remote expansion device
that allows the system to detect more complex and subtle movements. Sony launched Move, a handheld rod that uses both internal sensors and computer vision, via the Playstation Eye camera,
to track and interpret motion. And Microsoft shipped Kinect, a
sensor system that foregoes the controller entirely in favor of an
interface array of cameras and microphones capable of performing motion, facial, and voice recognition. By 2014 they had all
released updates or sequels, even though the original devices had
largely outworn their welcome. Shortly after shipping the Xbox
One, Microsoft unbundled the Kinect 2 hardware to enable the
company to reduce the system's price (and to answer for privacy
concerns about its always-on camera).

< 89 >

It's easy to blame the decline of gestural interfaces on trendiness and market forces, but perhaps unsophisticated, contrived design also bears some of the burden. Designers and players tend to understand gestural control as *actions*. Lean side to side on the Joyboard to ski in *Mogul Maniac*. Grasp and release the Power Glove to catch and throw in *Super Glove Ball*. Bat a hand in front of the EyeToy to strike a target in *EyeToy: Play*. Lean a plastic motorbike to steer in *Hang On*. Swing a Wii remote to strike a tennis ball in *Wii Sports*. Gestures of this sort also strive for realistic correspondence of the sort advocated by the direct manipulation human–computer interaction style. Input gestures, the thinking goes, become more intuitive and enjoyable when they better resemble their corresponding real-world actions. And games become more gratifying when they respond to those gestures in more sophisticated and realistic ways.

Such values drove the design of all the interface systems mentioned above: MotionPlus, Wand, and Kinect all involve high-resolution technologies that capture and understand movement in detail. Physical realism is the goal, a reduction of the gap between player action and in-game effect commensurate with advances in graphical realism. As one review of the more sophisticated Wii MotionPlus puts it, "It's like going from VHS straight to Blu-ray."[1] But even if physical realism might offer a promising direction for gestural interfaces, it is a value that conceals an important truth: in ordinary experience, gestures not only perform actions but also convey meaning.

Consider body language. A substantial portion of human communication takes place through nonverbal actions. Gestures like crossing one's arms, tilting one's head, and rubbing one's forehead telegraph important attitudes and beliefs. In these cases, gestures are intransitive; they do not perform actions. Instead they signal ideas or sensations: impatience, disbelief, weariness, and so forth. Other gestures take indirect objects. When we wave hello or flip someone the bird, we do not alter the physical environment in the same way a racquet does when striking a ball or a hand does when grazing a pool. We may, however, change how the recipient of the gesture thinks or feels about us or the world in general.

But gestures, be they transitive or intransitive, direct or indirect, can also alter our own thoughts or feelings about the world or ourselves. These sensations can be complex, and they can evolve. Flipping someone off may impress delight, then guilt, then shame. Reaching into a clogged drain may instill dread, then disgust, then relief.

Manhunt 2 for Wii implements gestures in this fashion. It's a game that spurred controversy upon release in 2007: it was nearly banned in several countries partly because it asked players to act out heinous acts of torture through physical actions. Yet the game's coupling of gestures to violent acts makes them *more*, not *less*, repugnant by implicating the player in their commitment. In *Manhunt 2*, we are meant to feel the power of antihero Daniel Lamb's psychopathy alongside our own disgust at it. It is a game that helps us see how thin the line can be between madness and reason by making us *perform* abuse.

But gestures in *Manhunt 2* are still descended from direct manipulation, swings and thrusts of a controller mapped roughly to a character's torture. For a subtler, richer example of player gestures that imbue meaning through representation and evocation rather than direct manipulation, we must consult a more unusual sort of game.

Brenda Romero's Train is a tabletop game, the first in a projected series of six that the veteran videogame designer hopes to use to address difficult subjects. Train's game surface is a window, some panes broken, with additional broken glass scattered atop the surface of the play area. Three railway tracks extend at oblique angles across the width of the window. The object of the game is to load yellow people tokens into boxcars and to move them from one end of the track to the other. Players roll dice to add passengers and move trains forward, and they draw cards to execute other actions, such as switching tracks, damaging a train, and derailing. Terminus cards on each track reveal each train's destination at the end of the game: Auschwitz or another Nazi concentration camp.

Because it exists in one edition only, far fewer people have played Train than have discussed it. When the game periodical *The Escapist* published coverage of Romero's discussion of her series at a 2009 conference in North Carolina, a number of readers (among them industry veterans Ernest Adams and Greg Costikyan) wondered if the game mostly offered a "shocker ending," to use Adams's words.[2] On first blush, the dread and disgust and horror Train dispatches may seem like a trick of implementation, not an experience delivered through the playing of the game itself. Yet when one actually plays Train or watches others play it, its emotional power shifts from the epiphany of its ending to the individual gestures that construct its play session—gestures that must necessarily be enacted to reach that finale.

For example, players may add people to their boxcars. It is a simple act, one that might entail pointing and clicking in a PC or console game. But to do so in Train, players must insert the wooden tokens into the narrow doorway of the model boxcar. How to accomplish this feat is entirely up to the player—you might leave the train on the track and attempt to insert the token into the side. Or you might pick up the entire car, godlike, and drop the token as if it were an insect. Adding additional tokens requires tilting or otherwise upsetting the car to make it possible to cram more people in. This is a disturbing experience, and players seem to alter their gestures of passenger loading and unloading as they better understand their implications. Removing passengers at the end of the track requires similar physical investment. The tokens barely fit through the boxcar doors, and removing them is difficult. It's hard to avoid picking up the boxcar and shaking it against an open palm to remove tokens.

The moral and historical significance of these gestures, individually and collectively, is not lost on Train players or spectators. The game not only forces the player to rough up people, it also forces you to *figure out how* to do so. In so doing, the sense of complicity that at first seems tied only to the game's ending creeps anxiously into every action the player performs. Simple, trivial acts like picking up game tokens or moving pieces along the board take on rich multiplicities of meaning in the minds of players and spectators alike thanks to the game's striking ambiguity. In this game, the action one performs is important *as such*, not just in relation to the outcome it produces.

The relevance of gameplay gestures can be found in aspects of Train that have little to do with the progress of gameplay. For example, sometimes players have the opportunity to remove tokens from opponents' boxcars. The game never tells the player what to do with these tokens, so one could just as easily hide them in a pocket, "saving" the victims, as one could return them to play. One might even choose a different method of removal in an attempt to signal contempt to an opponent, a gentle touch that says, implicitly, "let's stop."

The game's setup engenders gestural significance as well. At its start, the yellow tokens are lined up in rows at the side of the table. As players reach for people to stuff into their boxcars, these neat rows become disturbed, uneven. Even as a spectator, participants may find it difficult to resist "fixing" these disorderly lines of people, returning them to a more uniform and stable state. Here we find a gesture that bears meaning even if it is not consummated. The sinking feeling that accompanies it is palpable— one cannot help but admit that there is a measure of comfort in extreme order, and that such comfort is one tiny pebble in the foundation of fascism.

Even the game's rules impart gestural meaning. They are intentionally ambiguous, and players will find themselves referring back to them frequently. Romero managed to acquire an authentic SS typewriter for the game (complete with SS sigrune above the 5 key), which she used to type up the rules. These sheets are placed in the typewriter at the start of the game. To read or review them, players must get up and face the typewriter, turning its knobs to reveal the desired text or to remove the sheets. As one leans in to read the page or to handle the typewriter, game rules instantly become military orders. One cannot help but allow sensations of loyalty and treachery, pride and disgust to well up with each click of the typewriter platen.

Train proves that a *player*'s response to a gesture is at least as important as the way the *game* responds to such a gesture. But Train is a tabletop game, not a digital one. Is it even possible to translate the gestural ambiguity of such an experience into a video game?

The answer might be found not in Train's form but in its method. The game embraces ambiguity at every turn, refusing to connect any dots. It never makes an argument about the Holocaust. It never even takes a position on whether the efficient movement of people from station to terminus ought to be praised or condemned by its players, whether they should adopt the role of a Nazi officer in order to grasp his plight or reject it as morally reprehensible. Instead, the game creates a circumstance in which the gestures a player performs—lining up passengers, loading and unloading them, moving trains to a death camp—are allowed to reverberate uncomfortably.

One of Will Wright's contributions to game design is his elevation of ambiguity to a first-order design principle. Even in simulation-heavy games like *SimCity* and *The Sims*, players are afforded tremendous interpretative freedom as they imagine what's going on behind the walls of their buildings or in the minds of their sims. In simulation, abstraction doesn't just simplify implementation, it also affords richer experience.

The same is true of gestural interfaces. While increased physical realism might allow actions to become more faithful in their specificity, compelling significance doesn't necessarily come for free. Indeed, by abstracting a game's response to gestures, games of all kinds can allow the player a richer interpretative field. And in many cases, interpretation is more interesting than responsiveness. Consider a much less politically charged example: *Dance Dance Revolution. DDR*'s success as an arcade title comes partly from its honed responsiveness to simple player steps. But its life as a venue for public performance was born from the spaces the game didn't measure between steps, spaces players felt compelled to fill with improvised maneuvers of their own.

Train might then invite questions about the mad dash toward new and improved gestural technology. Wii MotionPlus, PlayStation Move, and Microsoft Kinect all assume that higher resolution and greater fidelity inputs will result in more compelling games. As consumer virtual reality arrives on the market, the same promises of sensory immersion drive its hope to complement or unseat traditional and gestural controllers for something more compelling. And they will, in part; certainly the precise physical properties of Train are intrinsic to the gestural meaning they impart. But the speed of development and release of new hardware platforms also offer excuses not to explore the tools we already have. Perhaps the souls of our games are to be found not in ever-better accelerometers and infrared sensors but in the way they invite players to respond to them. After all, Romero's work shows that games can make the inspiration of particular player movements their primary purpose, rather than a mere instrument for superficial realism.

12

The Long Shot

Heavy Rain shows why games must overturn the conventions of film if they hope to realize the dream of interactive cinema

The Soviet filmmaker and theorist Lev Kuleshov first suggested that *editing* is film's primary quality. His well-known "Kuleshov effect" seemed to prove the point: in the experiment, Kuleshov cut between the expressionless shot of a famous Russian silent film actor (Ivan Mozzhukhin) and a variety of other shots: a bowl of soup, a young girl in a coffin, a young woman reposed on a chaise. Even though the shot of Mozzhukhin's face remained identical with each cut, the audience made different assumptions about the meaning of his expression.

Kuleshov's influential pupil Sergei Eisenstein believed it, too, arguing that editing techniques (particularly montage) made it uniquely possible for cinema to link seemingly unrelated images through juxtaposition. The Soviets weren't alone in their reverence of editing. D. W. Griffith's early work made strong use of editing and crosscutting, for example. And as the years and then the decades passed, editing only increased in importance. Stanley Kubrik adopted Kuleshov's position more or less directly. Francis Ford Coppola has said this about the practice:

> The essence of cinema is editing. It's the combination of what can be extraordinary images, images of people during emotional moments, or just images in a general sense,

< 96 >

but put together in a kind of alchemy. A number of images put together a certain way become something quite above and beyond what any of them are individually.[1]

Indeed, editing has become an ever more important tool in filmmaking. The use of jump cuts (edits that disrupt the continuity of a sequence) and quick cuts (rapid edits that increase the pace of a sequence) have become ever more common and familiar as action films and television have increased creators' reliance on editing as a central cinematic aesthetic.

But generally, videogames don't have cinematic editing. They can't, because continuity of action is essential to interactive media. In fact, that continuity is so important that most games (3-D games, anyway) give the player direct control over the camera, allowing total manipulation of what is seen and from what vantage point.

Perhaps, if we're being particularly generous toward cinema, we could count shifts in fixed-camera views in games like *Heavy Rain* and *Metal Gear Solid* as a type of jump cut, since the action is disrupted rather than continuous. But in most of these cases, shifts in camera correspond only with changes in location, not changes in the way a videogame mediates the player's relationship to space or action or theme.

Survival horror games offer the best specimen of film-like editing in games. By holding the camera hostage rather than giving the player control over it, games like *Resident Evil* and *Silent Hill* remove the control needed to create tension and fear. The best example of this effect through camera editing alone might be *Fatal Frame 2*, which creates an effective sense of simultaneous familiarity and dread as the player moves through rooms of the possessed homes in a village.

In modern cinema, edits move action forward. Films are short compared with games, but more importantly, editing helps a filmmaker focus the viewer's attention on important plot elements through abstraction. For example, instead of showing a character get ready and leave for work, a few rapid quick cuts can communicate the same information more efficiently: closet door opens, fingers button shirt, hand grabs keys, car backs out of driveway.

Like many interactive narratives, the cinematic, murder-mystery videogame drama *Heavy Rain* appears to adopt the practice of filmic editing by allowing the player to control how sequences of narrative appear based on quick-time event (QTE) actions. In this respect, it follows in a long lineage of titles starting with 1983's laser-disc animated game *Dragon's Lair*. But that similarity is a foil. Instead, the most important feature of *Heavy Rain*, the design choice that makes it more important than any other game in separating from rather than drawing games toward film, is its rejection of editing in favor of prolonging.

Consider the game's first scene. The player not only must dress Ethan Mars piece by piece, but first he must get out of bed and take a shower. Stairs must be mounted and descended, one by one, with a deliberateness second only to that of *Shenmue*. Things get only more detailed from there: the player must help Ethan, an architect, do work by drawing portions of a building sketch in his home office. He must set the table. He must make coffee and move groceries.

One might argue that the slow pace of the game's prologue is meant to teach the player how to control the character and execute QTEs. But later in the game, the unedited nature of these actions becomes completely central to a scene's meaning.

In the game's second chapter, Ethan loses track of his son, Jason, in a crowded mall, a mistake that proves dire. After Ethan buys Jason a red balloon, the boy wanders off and the player (as Ethan) must find him. In this, the first of several excellent crowd sequences in the game, the confusion and crush of people give the player a real sense of panic as Ethan moves from upper to lower level in the mall, then across its packed floor and out the front door, following both incorrect and correct clues in the form of floating red balloons.

Narratively speaking, the scene is abysmal. It is forced and obvious and unbelievable, and questions abound: What ten-year-old begs for a balloon? How can such a slow-moving car fatally injure a child? Is Jason really so stupid as not to know how to cross the street? Why does Jason feel so compelled to leave his father in the first place? This is the scene that also inaugurated the "Press X to Jason" meme, in reference to several moments in which the player is invited to depress the PlayStation controller's X key in order to make Ethan shout for his son. The effect was meant to be dramatic, but in practice it feels mostly silly and contrived.

As it turns out, the player doesn't really need narrative success to appreciate how truly frenzied the scene feels. In a film, that frenzy would be best carried out through quick cuts: Ethan looking in different directions; a fast pan of the crowd, left and right; Ethan's movement through the mall concourse; a handheld first-person view down the escalators; more visually confused panning; a glimpse of a balloon; and then a cut to a different boy grasping it. In this context, too, shouts of "Jason!" would feel more natural and less absurd than those enacted by a player with few other choices.

But as anyone knows who has actually lost a child in a public place, even if only briefly, the central sensations of that experience are not rapidness but slowness. The slow panic of confusion and disorientation, the feeling of extended uncertainty as moments give way to minutes. The sound of each footfall and the neurosis of each head turn.

While its narrative fails to set up a credible reason for the chase, the chase itself captures this panic far more than a sequence of cinematic edits might do. If the edit is cinema's core feature, then *Heavy Rain* does the opposite: it lengthens rather than abridges. The mall scene is but a warm-up for one of the game's most successful experiments in retention: chapter 3, "Father and Son." It takes place two years after the previous chapter, and it's clear that Jason's death has all but undone Ethan. In his shoes, the player must pick up and drive Ethan's surviving son, Shaun, home from school. Home is revealed to be a run-down shack, its box-strewn living room implying that the aftermath of Jason's death has also involved the destruction of Ethan's marriage.

The game would clearly like the player to believe that this chapter will allow the player to alter its narrative based on decisions made on behalf of Ethan. A schedule is posted on the wall, detailing when Ethan should study, eat, and go to bed. If the player follows these, the "Good Father" PSN trophy is awarded, offering some undeniable textual evidence to place player choice at the apparent center of the sequence.

But once again, far more powerful ideas emerge from the scene's lack of cinematic editing rather than its abundance of cinematic plot. In one sequence, the player makes dinner for Shaun. Ethan sits as Shaun eats, his pallid face staring at nothing. Time seems to pass, but the player must end the task by pressing up on the controller to raise Ethan from his chair. The silent time between sitting and standing offers one of the only emotionally powerful moments in the entire game.

Ethan says nothing. What is he thinking about? Is he mulling over what he might have done differently two years earlier? Is he fantasizing about his estranged wife? Is he lamenting the detachment he had exhibited moments ago toward Shaun? Is he plotting his return to professional success?

The game gives us no answers, but it invites the player to consider all these and many more by refusing to edit the scene down into a few moments of silence save the pregnant sounds of plate scraping and chair dragging. The mental effort the player exerts in this scene alone is orders of magnitude more meaningful than all the Lls and R2s Xs and Os in the rest of the game.

Another, equally intense sequence follows soon after. Upon being tucked into bed, Shaun realizes that his favorite teddy bear is missing, and reminds his father than he can't sleep without it. Once more, the game extends rather than compresses the hunt for the plush toy, as Ethan pads gloomily through the dark house in search of it.

Once retrieving the teddy bear from atop the washing machine, another extended moment of reflection is possible, as the player is invited to consider the origin of the toy and what secret meaning it bears for Shaun, Ethan, and perhaps even Jason. Was it a gift received during better times? An old toy of Jason's that Shaun uses as a tiny memory palace? By refusing to cut the scene short, the game effectively floods the player with possible implementations of this plush symbol.

In cinema theory, editing is sometimes contrasted with mise-en-scène, the establishment of a scene through sets, props, blocking, and other nondialogic means. Mise-en-scène can communicate emotional intangibles through the repleteness of a setting. For example, a shot of a refrigerator emptied of all contents save beer and pickles or of a large room of a loft with a cold concrete floor both might convey a sense of loneliness or isolation.

It's clear that *Heavy Rain* uses mise-en-scène extensively: the visual situation of the mall (crowded) and the house (in disarray) helps orient the player toward the important actions of each respective chapter. But cinematic mise-en-scène still must be communicated through editing. In film, it usually offers abstract, often contrived characterization through single shots or a concrete, if backgrounded, focus on space through long takes.

But it is not mise-en-scène that makes the "Father and Son" chapter emotionally evocative. Rather, it is the necessary absence of any such attention-directing devices thanks to a lack of editing in the interactive game world. Cinematic shots of or through a scene are replaced by the weird, arbitrary movements that characterize 3-D videogames. In the context of *Counter-Strike* or *Gears of War*, this movement becomes one of orientation toward objectives. But in a dramatic title like *Heavy Rain*, editing's absence invites players to discover, reveal, or create a few lingering, pregnant moments. These moments carry the game's dominant payload.

A final moment of prolonging punctuates the chapter, cementing the technique's potential as a first-order principle of game design. After tucking Shaun into bed, Ethan leaves, deploying the slow-rotated thumbstick QTE to close the door softly. In a film, this is where a good editor would cut to the next scene, allowing the door's latch to signal a fade to black and then a transition to the next chapter, Scott Shelby's encounter with Lauren White.

But in *Heavy Rain,* another option prevails. Faced with the bittersweetness of the situation, the player might turn back toward the door and simply look on it, allowing the mixture of hope and despair inside Ethan to dance with each other uncomfortably.

Heavy Rain's creators and critics have discussed its accomplishments in bringing videogames closer to cinema, primarily by adding low-level interactivity and mild branching decisions to the thematic and narrative structure of traditional filmmaking. Such ideas have been around for twenty-five years at least, from laser-disc coin-op to CDi, and they have enjoyed peaks and valleys of critical and commercial success during that time.

But there is something far more interesting at work in *Heavy Rain*: its successful rejection of the primary operation of cinema. The game doesn't fully succeed in exploiting this power, but it does demonstrate it in a far more synthetic way than do other games with similar goals. If "edit" is the verb that makes cinema what it is, then perhaps videogames ought to focus on the opposite: extension, addition, prolonging. *Heavy Rain* does not embrace filmmaking but rebuffs it by inviting the player to do what Hollywood cinema can never offer: to linger on the mundane instead of cutting to the consequential.

It's something to let Ethan ponder as he leans against the railing of his motel balcony, watching the rain fall endlessly.

13

Puzzling the Sublime

Good puzzle games unearth the overwhelming vastness of infinity

It's hard to talk about abstract puzzle games, particularly about *why* certain examples deserve to be called excellent ones. We can discuss their formal properties, or their sensory aesthetics, or their interfaces. We can talk about them in terms of novelty or innovation, and we can talk about them in terms of how compelling they feel to play. But observations like these seem only to scratch the surface of titles like *Drop7* and *Orbital*. Can we talk about such games the way we talk about, say, *Bioshock* or *Pac-Man* or *SimCity*? Such games offer aboutness of some kind, whether through narrative, characterization, or simulation. In each, there are concrete topics that find representation in the rules and environments.

Indeed, it's hard to talk about abstract games precisely because they are not concrete. Those with more identifiably tangible themes offer some entry point for thematic interpretation. Chess, for example, clearly draws inspiration from military conflict, not only because of its historical lineage and mechanics of capture, but also thanks to its named, carved pieces. When a knight takes a pawn, it's easy to relate the gesture to combat.

Go is somewhat harder to characterize. As the philosophers Gilles Deleuze and Félix Guattari wrote of the game, "Go pieces, in contrast [to chess], are pellets, disks, simple arithmetic units, and have only an anonymous, collective, or third-person

< 103 >

function: 'It' makes a move. 'It' could be a man, a woman, a louse, an elephant."[1] Even if one can imagine a Go stone as a soldier or an elephant or a Walmart, the game is still fundamentally about territory: whoever captures more of it wins. Puzzles create more trouble. Some logical and mathematical puzzles, like the Three Utilities Puzzle, have clear subjects or storylines.[2] Others, like Sudoku, do not. Most often, puzzles are entirely conceptual in form, with concreteness a mere accident of presentation.

A jigsaw puzzle might have a landscape or a hamburger imprinted on its completed surface, but that subject bears no relation to the puzzle itself. It's just a skin that facilitates the job of construction. The same is true of some manipulable puzzles, like tangrams. Others, like peg solitaire and Rubik's cube, are entirely abstract, with no clear relation to any sort of worldly being or action.

Videogames have frequently inherited from the tradition of puzzles. Text and graphical adventures make use of logical puzzles, often ones that require manipulating items to unlock doors. And we have plenty of adaptations of traditional abstract board games. But it's really manipulable puzzles that have had the strongest influence on contemporary abstract games, and for good reason: spatial relations translate well, and videogames are good at manipulating objects in space. But a problem arises when we try to talk about abstract puzzle games critically. It's hard to perform thoughtful criticism on puzzles because they don't carry meaning in the way novels or films or oil paintings do. The peg solitaire set on the table at Cracker Barrel does not function as a religious text, for example.

One approach to understanding abstract artworks is to treat them as metaphors or allegories. In some cases, the art helps us out through its title. Marcel Duchamp's cubist painting *Nude Descending a Staircase* immediately reveals the multiperspectival, superimpositions of a human form in motion. The same goes for Piet Mondrian's famous final completed painting, *Broadway*

Boogie Woogie, which reflects, if abstractly, the bustle of New York City.

In other cases, no such help can be gleaned from the work itself, and viewers must seek their own interpretations. Such is the case with Mondrian's *Composition with Yellow Patch*, for example, which offers no interpretive handle in its title or on its canvas. Games rarely give much away through their titles, mostly because they don't have a strong genealogical relationship with the history of painting. Still, our interpretive capacity makes it possible to read meaning in anything if we choose.

Perhaps the best-known representational interpretation of an abstract puzzle game addresses the best-known such game: *Tetris*. In her 1997 book *Hamlet on the Holodeck*, Janet Murray described *Tetris* as "the perfect enactment of the overtasked lives of Americans."[3] Tetriminoes fall, like tasks to be completed, emails to be read, meetings to be attended. One must act quickly, or the onslaught will quickly overwhelm. But once checked, filed, or satisfied, the process just starts all over again. There is no escape, save inevitable defeat.

The critic Markku Eskelinen pugnaciously disputes Murray's account as absurd: "Instead of studying the actual game Murray tries to interpret its supposed content, or better yet, project her favourite content on it; consequently we don't learn anything of the features that make *Tetris* a game."[4] Eskelinen observes the curiosity in reading a Soviet game as an allegory for the American work ethic and offers that "it would be equally far beside the point if someone interpreted chess as a perfect American game because there's a constant struggle between hierarchically organized white and black communities, genders are not equal, and there's no health care for the stricken pieces."

Yet Murray's interpretation is entirely reasonable. From the perspective of literary or art criticism, she offers something essential: evidence from the work itself. The fact that the game was made behind the Iron Curtain doesn't matter; a work escapes the context of its creation and recombines with new interpretations in myriad unexpected ways (what the philosopher Jacques Derrida calls *dissemination*). Nobody can tell you what a work "really means," provided you can mount textual evidence to show that your interpretation is sensical.

The problem with the Murray/Eskelinen approach to abstract puzzle games is that one wants the game to function only narratively, and the other wants it to function only formally. Neither is exactly right without the other. The problem seems to be this: the "meaning" of an abstract puzzle game lies in a gap between its mechanics and its dynamics, rather than in one or the other.

In his eighteenth-century tome on aesthetics, the philosopher Immanuel Kant distinguishes between the *beautiful* and the *sublime*. He relates beauty to nonlogical, subjective aesthetic judgements about the form of things. He describes the sublime in terms of a relationship between the faculties of imagination and reason.

Kant characterizes two kinds of sublimity. The *mathematical sublime* is a feeling of boundlessness or vastness, as caused by reflections on the infinitely large.[5] A pyramid is an example of such a structure, one that cannot be wholly taken in, in a single gaze. The *dynamical sublime* describes the feeling of being overpowered.[6] This latter sense often comes from natural objects such as the face of a cliff over the sea or that of an enormous thunderhead. Sensations of the mathematical sublime arise from largeness; sensations of the dynamical sublime arise from fear.

The meaning of games like *Drop7* and *Orbital* are best understood in relation to the sublime, particularly the mathematical sublime.

Drop7 asks the player to drop discs emblazoned with a number from one to seven down the columns of a 7 × 7 grid. Gravity carries them until they reach bottom or stack atop other discs. If a disc's number matches the quantity of discs in a row or column (no matter their numbers), the matching disc disappears. Gray discs cannot disappear until they are unlocked to reveal a number. This is done by causing a numbered disc to disappear adjacent to the gray disc two times. Points are scored for each disappearing disc, with bonuses awarded for chains and board clears.

Much is left to chance in *Drop7*. The board starts with some discs already in place, and each disc the player must place is drawn randomly. In some cases, a convenient number appears, allowing the player to execute a planned chain or avoid a dangerous situation. In other cases, an undesirable disc forces the player to change plans. Furthermore, when gray discs appear, their contents remain unknown to the player until surrounding discs reveal them. All together, these mechanics require the player to reassess the state of the board each turn. Gray discs can be taken as uncertainties, but doing so is unwise. It's much smarter to assume the worst of hidden numbers and plan accordingly.

Yet, even then, each turn requires a total reassessment of the state of the board based on the last turn's results and the present disc. While emergent consequences exist in chess and Go, *Drop7* makes the long-term impact of a single move visible even to the amateur player. The experience of playing *Drop7* is thus one of planning present moves against contingent future ones, given a set of slowly changing uncertainties. The vastness of possible moves is calculable for a moment, until it is disrupted by the randomness of new information. This is where the player finds the game's mathematical sublimity.

Mastery of the game is always temporary, as each move collapses the innumerable possibilities that exist before a disc drops into the fixity of a new situation just after. Yet, unlike the constantly changing dynamics of a chess or Go board, each move in *Drop7* reveals something more about itself later on, as previously unknowable impacts begin to exert torsion on the present.

In *Orbital*, the player fires orbs from a rotating gun at the bottom of the playfield. These orbs ricochet off walls and one another, until inertia stops them. Once stopped, the orbs grow until they touch a playfield wall or another ball. The player's goal is to break the orbs by striking them three times with new ones (a large counter on each ball shows the current hit count), scoring a point.

However, should an orb bounce such that it passes a white line just above the player's gun, the game is over. Following its cosmic theme, the orbs in play create gravitational fields that alter the path of subsequent ones.

Like *Drop7*, players of *Orbital* suffer an environment dependent on the increasing contingency of aggregate moves. One tactic for play involves estimating the trajectories of orbs based on the friction and gravity of the environment. One can, for example, attempt to lodge a cluster of small orbs in the corners, increasing the likelihood of destroying many with a single shot. Yet, as each orb settles, it alters the gravity well of a part of the playfield, effectively erasing whatever understanding the player had developed about the earlier topology. Notably, this same disorientation occurs even when the player succeeds, since an exploded orb alters local gravity, too.

In *Drop7,* the mathematical sublime enters the game through chance: the random generation of discs under the gray coverings and in the player's hand. In *Orbital,* there is no chance whatsoever. Every move in the game is calculable. But the vastness of the ever-changing universe makes such planning impossible for the human player, who must win out over both timing and physics to carry out a shot intentionally, whether or not it was well-planned in the first place. *Orbital* is unforgiving. While *Drop7* slowly winnows down choice until the player is overcome by failure, *Orbital* puts failure on the screen, a thin, fragile line subject to even the lightest graze.

To play *Drop7* or *Orbital* is to practice string theory, to assess the unknown branches of infinite futures. Whether one plays effectively or not, these games force players to reflect on the mathematical boundlessness of the systems that drive them, systems that alter themselves with every move.

Can we say that *Drop7* and *Orbital* are "about" something? And if so what? Here it is useful to return to Murray's interpretation of *Tetris*. One might find a similar mathematical sublimity at work in the latter game, after all. Each block alters the topology of the playfield, the player must alter that topology to continue the game, and chance dictates what pieces might be available to consummate the geometrical promises made earlier. But *Drop7* and *Orbital* differ from *Tetris* in an important way: they are turn-based, not continuous. The player must always intervene to make the next move, offering an opportunity to reflect on the enormousness of the task, a requirement of sublimity.

When Murray reads *Tetris* as a game about the Sisyphean toil of work, she refers not to the game's dynamics of mathematical sublimity but to the temporal dynamics of its operation. And time, as it happens, is precisely the formal explanation Eskelinen offers after his rebuff of Murray's narrativism. Office work is generally not a variety of sublimity like the rapidly branching parallel worlds of *Drop7* and *Orbital,* but it is often an experience of time's arrow, of unstoppable progression, with or without progress.

In *Tetris,* the method of play disrupts access to the sublime. But in *Drop7* and *Orbital,* the player's pondering of and reaction to sublimity is enhanced by the mode of action. Arrested between each move, it is possible to allegorize that sensation, taking it as the subject of the game. For example, *Drop7* offers an experience of dread and smallness in the face of unpredictability—not only of the future (the disc to be placed), but also of the past (the unrevealed gray discs). Such an experience feels much like that of, say, personal choice. Should one contribute to the Red Cross? Convert to Islam? Take a mistress?

To be sure, the surface and model of *Drop7* do not feel like this at all, but the *experience* of mathematical sublimity is alike in both cases. In this respect, one might argue that *Drop7* is more about moral choice than are games like *Fable* or *Bioshock.* The latter titles may simulate the actions of decision, but just like *Tetris* does for work, they do not capture the theme of choice through dynamics.

Orbital builds on this theme, but toward a different end. Absent chance, *Orbital's* subject revolves around placement. Even given the full knowledge of the physical dynamics of the universe (a subject that finds its way into the game's visual theme), the human player is still too fallible to succeed at such placement over time. Even the master will be found wanting. Such an interpretation of these games, one among many, cannot be gleaned from game mechanics or from the dynamics those mechanics produce. Instead, they take form in the allegorical exhaust of player sensations between the two.

Good puzzle games can do many things. But to call them "good" based on properties of addictiveness or depth or elegance—the common values used to judge titles like *Tetris* and *Drop7* and *Orbital*—is to say that abstract games can exert only cold, formal effects on their players. The sublime is just the opposite of cold formalism: a feeling of overwhelm, of vastness, of abundance. The sublime helps us see the limits of our own reason, showing us the instability and immensity of the world. Surely such a theme hasn't been exhausted by a few games about blocks and numbers and shapes, just as it hasn't been captured by a few games about war or sacrifice or loss. The role of the mathematical sublime in puzzle games should give us pause about our goals as creators and critics. We look for masterpieces in games by comparing them with familiar works of representational art, like film, painting, and literature. But the sublime is found elsewhere: in architecture, in nature, in weather. Perhaps we should look to these sources for inspiration, too.

14

Work Is the Best Place to Goof Off

Simulations used to celebrate realism. Now they help us
see the space between reality and videogames.

A 1982 tagline for *Microsoft Flight Simulator* boasted, "If flying
your IBM PC got any more realistic, you'd need a license." The
quip was meant to appeal to real pilots and those who fancied
themselves armchair aviators.

I was neither but played *Flight Simulator* anyway. Well, "play"
is a generous word for it. I loaded and manipulated its interfaces.
To say that I simulated flight would be an overstatement. And in
that sense, the 1982 advert rings true: *Flight Simulator* was realistic enough that it became as unyielding as would a small craft
cockpit in my inexpert hands. Playing *Flight Simulator* was more
like admiring the idea that someone could play *Flight Simulator,*
much like traveling by aircraft amounts to the admiration that
engineers can design and build airplanes and pilots can successfully operate them.

The term *simulator* has a complex rhetorical history. Many
simulators have nothing to do with interactive entertainment—
military and commercial equipment are often simulated in both
ordinary software and complex, purpose-built hardware for training purposes. In these cases, *simulator* suggests realism and detail and professionalism and seriousness. In the serious games
community, which creates and deploys games for uses in corporate, governmental, or organizational contexts, calling games
simulations often apologizes for or ends around the negative

< 111 >

associations games have in officialdom. A game is a plaything, a distraction, a waste of money, a waste of time. "Why are you wasting taxpayer money on *games*?" can quickly be converted into "Look at how the government is using *simulations* to save money on training and preparedness."

Simulators are everywhere, it turns out, but nobody notices. Military and aviation simulators are well-known, but even more common are the vehicular simulators typically used in the design and engineering of cars, trucks, motorcycles, and other motorized apparatuses. Medical simulators offer mechanical or computational re-creations of the human body for the development of adeptness in a particular procedure, whether it be common like CPR or specialized like endoscopy. In each case, cost, complexity, safety, and expertise drive the desire to deploy simulation. And those considerations underscore the serious purpose of simulation. To call a game a *simulation* is always in part to divorce it from the excesses of enjoyment and to send it to work.

But in entertainment games, simulators take on another, more surprising quality: they signal a disruption between the realism of commercial simulation and the abstraction of videogames. A simulator isn't just a more detailed or a more realistic or a more professional ludic rendition of a particular subject. It's also a game that resists the genteel abstractions of ordinary entertainment. Flying a plane takes work, expertise, care, and attention to detail. While plenty of games share those values (*FIFA* or *League of Legends* could hardly be accused of failing to embrace them), fewer do so with respect to flight. The promise one assumes from a simulation is not really that of detail or comprehensiveness, even if those terms are often used to advertise them, but of resistance to abstraction. Where an ordinary game would remove the boring parts, a simulator would celebrate them.

Against all odds in the era of pay-to-win mobile games and stylized open-world titles, simulators have experienced a resurgence. Dozens of such games have appeared in recent years, on store shelves as much as on Steam: *Train Simulator. Airport Simulator. Farm Simulator. Car Mechanic Simulator. Skyscraper Simulator.*

Most of these games offer some variety of a career mode, allowing players to advance in their chosen expertise, which typically involves the day-to-day activity of a mundane profession.

These new simulator games all derive from the original model of *Microsoft Flight Simulator,* a game that sat squarely between tool and entertainment. Most embrace and acknowledge that influence, even if only by adopting the characteristic thin, oblique typography of *Flight Simulator'*s title. But in practice, these new simulators reveal a more complex relationship between the ease and facility of games and the austerity of simulators. They are less simulations of their chosen subjects than representations of the unexplored design space between simulators and games.

Take *Euro Truck Simulator 2,* a commercial trucking game. It offers the usual invitation to a career in freight hauling, but the primary experience of the game is that of driving a tractor-trailer across the cities and countrysides of Europe. For those accustomed to driving in games like *Grand Theft Auto* or *Watch Dogs,* the most notable experience in *Euro Truck Simulator* is that of having to stay in the lanes, avoid collisions, and follow basic traffic laws. Such activities are not optional as they might be in an open-world game, since infractions and vehicle damage severely affect the player's ability to drive the truck and, thereby, to play the game.

But as much as this enforcement of basic rules of the road implements the idea of inhospitableness in simulators, the game also betrays that promise. Finicky controls and slightly caricatured physics make driving your euro truck difficult, such that even the smallest jostle might send the enormous machine lurching, rag-doll style, into the railing. To play *Euro Truck Simulator 2* is not to play a simulator so much as it is to play the difference between a simulator and game, to toe the line between.

Surgeon Simulator offers an even clearer example. The game's title suggests officialdom and seriousness, the sort of tools one would expect hospitals or medical schools to invest hundreds of thousands of dollars in when taking a long view on operating room success and efficiency. But in truth, the title couldn't be farther from the serious game its title suggests. Instead, *Surgeon*

Simulator foregrounds the awkward, impossible reality of controlling a doctor's fine motor gestures in the context of the operating room. It does so by taking advantage of well-developed game technologies and design patterns that have never really worked very well in videogames despite being incredibly popular.

Physics has long been a part of games, and the simulation of the physical world, either in abstraction for entertainment or through accuracy for scientific or training purposes, remains a cornerstone of creating and operating games. Modern game engines all provide some version of physical simulation "for free," which is just to say, game designers and programmers can often add rigid- and soft-body physical simulations by checking a few boxes. But physics means something quite particular and peculiar in the context of games.

To some extent, physics is a kind of special effect, as in the case of particle systems. This computer graphics display technique uses a large number of small visual elements to simulate the appearance of a larger phenomenon, such as fire, smoke, clouds, fog, dust, and so forth. Given modern 3-D computer games' penchant for both dark, brooding environments and fiery explosions, this kind of physical simulation is far more relevant in a game than it might be in the more ordinary scenario, such as an operating room.

Unlike particle systems, rigid- and soft-body physics applies to almost everything we encounter in the ordinary world. Your feet against a soccer ball; your tires in contact with the pavement; a scalpel severing the flesh of a patient on the operating table; a dish plunging into the soapy water in a kitchen sink. In our ordinary lives, these dynamics are nested and complex, such that intuition and experience make it difficult to fully characterize all the factors at play in a particular physical experience.

Even with far greater processing power than is currently available, videogames couldn't possibly hope to re-create the entire world at the most granular physical level, in real time. And so they abstract. A vehicle's weight and force and lift stand in for its overall performance. A ball or projectile's trajectory is dampened by an abstraction of its in-flight alterations thanks to wind or its drag once deposited on grass or snow. The result is that distinctive feeling of "game physics" we have come to know so well. It helps us distinguish one vehicle from another in *Watchdogs*. It offers something resembling the physical sensation of walking waist-deep in water or sludge in *The Last of Us*. And of course, it affords the pleasure and confusion of the physical collision, interaction, and destruction of objects in *Half-Life* or *Unreal*.

It is here, at the point where physics becomes realistic enough that it induces awe, that a game like *Surgeon Simulator* steps in to throw things asunder—literally. For the same physical assumptions that make it possible to explode walls and knock crates off ledges also make the ordinary, everyday experience of the physical world in games preposterous and absurd. In most games, the small-scale objects that fill desks and cabinets are locked in place, accessed by button press or else represented as textured objects that resist interaction. But these are precisely the sorts of tools that a surgeon—that greatest and noblest of precision actors—must contend with at the level of intricate action.

Surgeon Simulator juxtaposes the conventions of videogame rigid- and soft-body physics with the reality of surgical precision at the level of individual digits accessing and manipulating tools and tissues. In the PC version of the game, the mouse controls the virtual surgeon's hand (his name is Nigel Burke). Holding the right button allows the player to rotate the hand at the wrist, and keyboard presses provide the ability to open or close the joints of individual digits for grasping and manipulation.

The result is a send-up of the idea of a surgical simulator. Instruments and canisters (and, occasionally, entire human organs) go flying about, dutifully obeying the rigid-body physics simulation so common as to be deeply integrated into modern game engines. The difficulty of controlling Burke becomes the point of the game rather than its failure. But to say that the game is about surgery—let alone "simulating" surgery—is to take many steps too far. Rather, *Surgeon Simulator* is a game about the ludicrousness of *all* physical interactions in *all* modern videogames. After all, every game makes more or less the same assumptions about the level of abstraction necessary to represent the physical world. Those assumptions become ideologized, and we cease to think about them—even as we often have the (correct) sense that physical objects and substances are being caricatured for our benefit in videogames.

In large part, we are *always* flopping our way toward victory in games, even in games that reject the intrinsic humor and stupidity of that floundering in favor of the seriousness of dark, gritty underworlds in which square-jawed men fire projectiles at walls just to see them crumble.

Creators and players seem to be aware of the strange new design space opened by modern "simulators" and revel in occupying it. A new genre that we might name "non-simulators" has emerged, notable for claiming to be simulators by name while explicitly rejecting the premise of realism and detail in practice. The best-known title is *Goat Simulator,* in which players destroy an environment by means of a goat. And *Rock Simulator 2014* offers players the opportunity to "watch beautiful rocks in any location in the world." Both titles were born as jokes, but a marketplace of earnestly engaged players nevertheless has emerged around them. Why? It seems safe to conclude that players don't really want to simulate goats and rocks—especially since neither activity is supported by the games. Instead, players of this new crop of simulators want to experience the wilderness where games haven't previously dared to settle. Strangely, this is what *simulator* now seems to mean: a thing that knows it's not a game in the customary sense, but which isn't a scientific or professional apparatus either. Soon enough, this sense of simulator may overtake the previous notion of a serious, scientific apparatus. A simulator will have become a work that shows the intrinsic impossibility of representing a chosen subject with playable computer graphics, rather than computation's inevitable mastery of the physical world.

15

A Trio of Artisanal Reviews

The open-world exploration game *Proteus*
served three ways

1. Nil Person

Videogames are narcissistic. They are about you, even when they put you in someone else's shoes. You are a space marine among hell spawn. You are a mafioso just released from prison. You are a bear with a bird in your backpack. You are a Tebowing Tim Tebow. We may think we play videogames to be someone or something else, but inevitably we do so to be ourselves as well—ourselves in the guise of someone else.

Film and television and literature may not put you in control like games do, but instead they put you outside, forcing you to take seriously the fact that the characters are *not* you but someone else. Sometimes being in control is too facile, too misleading. Does piloting *Uncharted*'s Nathan Drake from ledge to ledge lead to any greater understanding of his opaque motivations than watching *House of Cards*' equally impenetrable Frank Underwood? If agency means click-guessing *The Walking Dead*'s Lee Everett around his family drugstore, then maybe passivity is underrated.

Even games without embodied, playable first- or third-person human characters or their synecdoches are still about "you." In *Tetris* or *Drop7* or *Osmos,* you are not anyone. Rather, "you" are the pretend god in control of a manipulable world on which meaningful force can be exerted. These are not games you might

< 117 >

be likely to reconstruct out of paper or mashed potatoes, but you could if you set your mind to the task. They are tiny universes in which you are the prime mover, even if not the designer. You are the player, and without you the game grinds to a halt.

It's tempting to see *Proteus* as just another first-person art game, one that starts with conventional keyboard-and-mouse shuffle-looking and then strips away other verbs like "jump" and "shoot." Only movement remains, along with the obstreperous spacebar command to "sit," as if giving the finger to all those games in which sitting would result in an immediate bloodbath.

Many will dismiss *Proteus* on these grounds, concluding that it is "not a game," before launching into some tired tirade about the proper properties of genuine games: goals, choices, victory, what have you. Those players have been successfully provoked. *Proteus* intends the provocation, but doesn't do enough to follow through on it. At question is not whether the game offers sufficient choice or challenge to deserve the name "game," but *whose* choice or challenge is presented in the first place.

It's not the gameplay that's missing from *Proteus*. Rather, it's the *you*, the agent who would partake of it. Or, at least, in *Proteus* you are not the *you* you are used to.

The game loads. At first you think that you are on a boat, or some sort of vessel anyway. You look around. A misty island appears in the distance, *appears* because you can see it. You can hear the lapping water. The horizon seems to bob along to match your movements and your shifting perception. You move and look, exploring the sea, the beach, the hill, the mountain.

But there was no boat. It should have been your first clue, like the obvious sign at the start of an M. Night Shyamalan film, the blatant hint that gives away the twist before you knew there was one. What can rest unperturbed on water and on earth, but still move nimbly? A specter. A miniature hovercraft. Jesus of Nazareth.

Things get weirder on land. Traversing *Proteus* feels familiar, banal even. Not the space, the island itself, but the traversal.

Moving, looking—you've done it all before, inside Castle Wolfenstein, on Bob-omb Battlefield, in Rapture. But something's off this time, something subtle. Different terrains can be traversed without distinction. Hills and summits can be ascended smoothly and without struggle no matter their incline. From a distance, you see a snowcapped mountain and devise a tactic for reaching its summit. But your plan is quickly proved superfluous, as contact with the peak's foothill results in an immediate, quick assent, as if by invisible funicular.

What to make of it? Dismay, at first, even anger. Perhaps the creators of *Proteus* were too lazy or too inept to craft a more sophisticated locomotion system, opting instead just to couple a default camera view to first-person controls, an abstract cursor in an environment.

But this obvious analysis is also the wrong one. Rather than conclude that the work is incomplete or ill-conceived, why not instead assume that it means to be exactly what it is and that it issues a challenge to those who might interact with it: to form credible theories about why it is the way it is, rather than criticisms about why it is not something else.

There is no "you" in *Proteus*, at least not in the way you thought there was. There is only an island. The experience you have on that island isn't an experience *on* an island, at all. Instead, it's an experience *of* an island. An island's experience. *Proteus* is a game about being an island instead of a game about being on one.

What does an island do? Not much, on a human scale. Islands are accreted from submarine vulcanism over hundreds of thousands of years, as tectonic plate directions shift to yield protrusions in solid, dense rock. The Big Island of Hawaiʻi is young at some half a million years old. The oldest seamount in the Hawaiian-Emperor chain, Mejii Seamount, is at least eighty million years old.

Proteus spares us the obvious portrayals of geological time, of hot spots on the Earth's mantle, of lava flows and shield building and erosion, of scientific educationalism. Such features are not really of the island, after all, but of its creation. Just as Nate Drake isn't the same as his ontogeny from zygote to fetus to infant, so being *Proteus* isn't the same as its simulated, abstracted geological formation.

As for "exploration," such is the game's clever conceit, the ruse that tricks you into thinking the work is about *you,* into thinking that you are there at all. *Proteus* meets you partway, offering the appearance of changes in movement, of changes in view, of the ability to "sit." But these are just metaphors, the minimum necessary invitation to provide you, the human player, a satisfactory analogy through which to grasp the island's existence as island. The arbitrary configurations of a computer interface, whose careless tousles along a 3-D vector happen to correspond with the usual manner in which a player might navigate a virtual world. One explores *Proteus* less like one explores a wooded nature preserve and more like one explores a naked body—by moving it through one's attention rather than by moving one's attention through it.

In *Proteus,* we find something in between the personal time of human agency and the historical time of tectonic effects. Day and night don't pass so much as the island dresses in day and night's clothing. Night doesn't descend on the island so much as *the island nights,* like the squirrel scurries or the leaves fall. If tousled in the right way, it relents, donning the garb of different seasons. Time doesn't pass on it any more than you move around it. It is you who is too dense, too stuck in your own ape body that you require time to pass before your senses kick in.

Islands. They are a common staple of videogames: *Myst, Uncharted, The Secret of Monkey Island.* Yet we don't think much about these islands themselves. Even in a game like *Far Cry,* in which the environment has a much larger role to play, that environment is still rendered *for you,* you the playable character and for you the human player. *Proteus*'s island isn't for *you* at all. It isn't concerned with your attention span or your expectations. It's just there. Just there, until it gets bored and turns you off.

2. Traveler

It was springtime in *Proteus* when I visited. Spring is strange there: the trees dump pink and yellow petals onto the ground. I think they were petals; it's hard to tell in *Proteus,* where everything looks foreign.

Imagine the most improbably regular autumn, in which leaves tumble from branches along a regular rhythm rather than in tandem with the environment, in which physics is reduced to mere downness. Now imagine that the leaves are pink and that the tree canopies bear no foliage, only petals. Floral kudzu, taking over.

Are there even trees underneath, I began to wonder, or only the form of trees? Scaffolds, maybe, the twisted mess of iron detritus to which, for whatever reason, petals have attached. The remains of the island of Myst, or of the planet Sera millennia hence.

As a place to visit, *Proteus* is beyond alien. Unworldly rather than otherworldly. Its apparent familiarity defies that otherness at first, like roads and touring buses might do in Kyoto or Khartoum. You've seen it all before, you'll think when you arrive, and you won't be wrong. But you visit *Proteus* to see what clouds and flowers look like *in Proteus,* not to replace sights you could find just as easily at home. In Kuala Lumpur, you eat Nasi Lemak rather than steak and eggs; in Proteus, billboard trees spill flora and tousle pixel-beetles. It's just how things are.

When you stop to think about it, it's strange that we consider travel a kind of leisure, that we talk about taking time off for it, that we call it vacation. Travel is a lot of work, after all. Not just the process of voyaging, the cars and carparks and the airports and such, but also the process of being in your destination. Finding your way around the streets and the countryside. Learning some of the language, finding a comfortable café. Taking in the pedestrian mall and the art museum. It's exhausting.

Proteus is no different. Transiting the island is both effortless and arduous, like taking the Métro across the small diameter of Paris. Effective and ready to hand, yet meandering and inefficient.

Try not to look like a tourist, WASDing around to get your bear-
ings, or following the dirt path etched through the grass toward
the abandoned hut. It will disappoint, like all places of interest.
You'll have to get acclimated on your own. There is no "tutorial"
for Oslo or Ottawa, why should *Proteus* have one?

Eventually, all travel ceases to surprise us. It doesn't take long.
Even on a short trip to somewhere unfamiliar, the diner you chose
for breakfast the first day can become stifling by the third. But
returning to a once-foreign place as it becomes familiar offers
new depths. Transiting confidently from Charles de Gaulle to St.
Michel Notre Dame by RER, then walking to the hotel you meant
to choose rather than the one you guessed about. Knowing which
way to turn when you alight from an exit chosen deliberately at
Odéon rather than Cluny–La Sorbonne. These small gestures become an experienced traveler's triumphs.

Most places change slowly, so expert travel entails one of two
options: returning frequently or lingering for an extended stay.
And just as its petals and paths betray convention, so *Proteus*
makes unusual demands.

In one sense, returning isn't possible: *Proteus* procedurally
generates itself anew with each visit, so no two trips fall on familiar soil. Yet every version of *Proteus* presents an identifiable
rendition, borrowing a page from Italo Calvino's Kublai Khan: "I
have constructed in my mind a model city from which all possible
cities can be deduced." Each rendition is not so unfamiliar as to
be wholly foreign, just as each district of an unfamiliar city still
subscribes to an overall plan. In this sense, *Proteus* is not very
protean; what changes is incidental.

Yet, since getting your bearing and finding your way are so
central to your visit, the utility of familiarity melts away. Would
Manhattan still be Manhattan if each face of its rectilinear blocks
were torn asunder and reattached to one another at random? Yes,
in a way, but it would take some getting used to. In the process,
you might discover new watering holes or green grocers or parks
or bodegas or buskers thanks to having your routine disrupted.

Such is what it feels like to return to a new generation of *Proteus*, where one keeps an eye out for previously unseen wildlife instead of previously unseen gastropubs.

Still, one can evade doomsday in *Proteus* by saving a "postcard" for later. Pressing a key in-world takes an abstract screen capture that embeds your visit's state in its pixel data. You can return later or share the image (and its embedded world) with others. We once went on safari to hunt animals, then to capture them on film. Now in *Proteus* you can capture the world around animals on disk.

Lingering comes more naturally than return. On a visit to an unfamiliar place, there comes a point at which everything snaps into place. In most cases, that moment is conceptual; it's in your head. Time and traffic and tacos pass around and through you, and eventually after enough of it, clarity overtakes confusion.

But *Proteus* makes this familiarity real, or material at least. A part of the landscape. Time advances in *Proteus*, too, in the sense that day turns to night and back to day again. Personal time, anyway; historical time just lingers.

Eventually, some visitors to *Proteus* will find a way to move beyond the eternal spring. Growing familiar with Prague or Peoria is a matter of persistence, to be sure, but not much more than that. Simply being there with intention is enough, and it pays dividends. By contrast, lingering in *Proteus* takes more than persistence. It takes a certain kind of looking and listening for time to progress beyond days and into seasons. A *particular* kind; there is only one, and it has to be decoded. In this sense, *Proteus* is more like *Myst* than it first seems: eventually, only one path opens. Cities don't have solutions, but *Proteus* does, in a way.

Summer was pleasant, but I have to admit that I began racing through autumn, which was bleak and soggy rather than vivid and crisp. By winter, I wished I hadn't stayed so long. Something was not quite right. The petals were gone, the dragonflies and the frogs, too. Just blue blueness, the simulated night reflecting off the simulated snow. The galaxy buzzing instead of the dragonflies.

The theory of alien archaeology resurfaced. In retrospect, if the trees aren't trees, then why would the petals be petals? The best I can say in full confidence is that they are pink, and square. Pure pinkness and pure squareness, pure rectilinear-roseness, as if borrowed from a James Turrell installation, tumbling to the ground (I'll call it the ground) and infecting the soil with pink as well, spreading like love or like sickness.

Then something happened, and my trepidation seemed warranted. I was reflecting on the fact that the flowers were even more unearthly than I had previously realized when my trip came to an unexpected end. You'll have to see it for yourself. Cities don't have spoilers, but *Proteus* does, in a way.

I suppose every trip is a trip to nowhere. Don't you secretly fantasize that your vacation to Fiji or San Francisco will be the last visit—not just your last, but anyone's? Doomsday is the only day worth dreaming. Normally it's impossible; someone always stays behind. But not in *Proteus*. Nothing lingers, except those postcards you captured to show off later. Don't worry, *Proteus* helpfully offers a button to reveal their containing folder, so you can delete them.

3. Habitat Modulation

Imagine a radio made out of a world. What would you tune in? The rain, maybe. The stochastic dance of its droplets. Rrr rr rr rr r r. I like it best when it strengthens enough to chime against the windowpanes. Fluid fingernails on the glass.

Sound fills spaces. It's called *diffusion,* the spreading of sonic energy in a physical environment. Perfectly diffusive spaces share the same acoustic properties all throughout. Such settings have to be engineered, whether architecturally like a carefully designed concert hall or prosthetically through the addition of sound diffusors like one finds in a recording studio.

Most spaces aren't so purposefully designed; they are "nondiffusive," which is just to say, ordinary. You configure your home theater to offer an ideal listening space around your couch. You lean in, struggling to hear your dinner companion because the restaurant was designed to maximize liveliness around your table rather than to optimize conversation at it.

In our daily lives, we shift constantly among different sonic domains. Our bias toward visual culture means that usually we see that transition more than we hear it, but careful attention can help attenuate visual in favor of auditory sensation. Instead of seeing a morning made up of house, yard, car, if you squint a bit you can hear one made of kettle, birds, engine, NPR Morning Edition.

Sometimes you have to close your eyes to hear. So overwhelming is the visual sensorium, and so central to our social lives. We close our eyes to calm ourselves because it's so hard to focus on our inner thoughts with so many outer influences pouring in. The guru does not advise the meditation practitioner to cover the ears but to close the eyes, at least temporarily—to reset the dynamic energy of vision, but not so much as to fall into slumber.

You probably do this more often than you realize, but still not often enough. Morning again. The door latches behind you, leaving behind the thud of children's feet, the clank of the dishwasher, the chatter of Matt Lauer. Instead: a deep breath, the swoosh of nearby leaves, the whir of a distant lawnmower. A small moment lost among larger moments, but precious for its modesty. Like seeing the big eyes of a small child, hearing the wind beetle through leaves draws out vice from the chest and spreads it across the skin, where it burns and then evaporates.

Such moments are rarer than they could be. You might visit the woods behind the park or drive out to the nature preserve or the beach, or the shopping mall even, but such propositions are too inconvenient to become habits.

We've tried to domesticate them: fireplaces, aquaria, the white-noise generators that take the place of alarm clocks in mid-range hotel rooms: gentle rain, crashing surf, babbling brook. But these aren't meant to be heard, just to mask out other sounds until boredom or slumber overtakes them.

Proteus offers an alternative: a sonic device one uses by moving through its spatial landscape and its temporal fluxes. If a toy like a Spirograph is used to produce complex mathematical curves by manipulating its far simpler physical apparatus, then a world like *Proteus* is used to produce complex sonic configurations in the same manner.

Exploring *Proteus* is also an optical experience, of course. The game presents a rendered 3-D environment that facilitates navigation. But its imprecise, indeterminate visual style invites the player to de-emphasize the usual desire for scintillation through visual verisimilitude in favor of listening for desirable auditory configurations. One moves through *Proteus* not to see but to arrange a particular kind of hearing.

At first this is rough going. All you hear are random sounds, a cacophony of electronic tones and noise. A jumble. A weird mismatch, too: a pastoral nightclub run by pixel cupcakes. But it's just the surprise of auditory novelty, like the first sonic deluge of New York City to the novice ear. Eventually patterns emerge; or rather, you become able to produce sonic patterns by orchestrating your movements. *Proteus* is an island you tune like a radio. Or maybe, a radio that looks like an island.

What's playing? Spring-night-rain-meadow-fireflies. An oscillating whistle of the insects along with the sprinkle of rain, which slowly subsides as the clouds pass, giving way to the pure tone of digital owls.

The nuisance of the sunrise, whistling flutelike. It's worse than the alarm clock's klaxon, but like the latter you cannot escape it. Just wait it out, let the rosy dawn give way to cyan and the flutes to frequency-oscillating sine tones.

Seeking respite from the din. A tall mountain on this run of *Proteus*, blanched by snow and beset with the silence of dead goblin trees on one side. The wind. Finally the throbbing ebbs. Too soon really, it becomes stifling in turn. A tall castle's keep without surrounding battlements presents itself at the opposite end of the peak, radiating abstract, oscillating squawks. The wind sounds cold when married to it.

Finding a frog or a brace of ducks. In *Proteus* safari is not just a matter of seeing a new creature but of mixing it down with the background tracks, of dancing with the bounce of square amphibians and semicircular fowl. Then lingering with the frog until night falls, when it sings a rhythmic, fizzy ballad if undisturbed. Every channel is synesthesia and mixed metaphor. Summer is syncopated flowers. Autumn draws itself out, but still jingles with the bells of leafiness. Those chimes don't represent the leaves like the droplets represent the rain, no more than the French horns represent clear skies. Rather, to hear the horns, escape the rain. Just before daybreak autumn creaks like a boat. Winter's midnight jingles like the paralyzing ghost of an alien carnival where, years ago, an almond-eyed daredevil was decapitated.

A music visualizer does just what its name suggests: it makes music visible by transforming an audio input's frequency spectrum into parameters for a moving image. You've seen them in WinAmp and in iTunes, and in Jeff Minter's Neon light synthesizer in the Xbox 360. But *Proteus* is not a music visualizer. It does not present a visual, traversable representation of a musical composition. Rather, it is a habitat receiver that can be tuned in for sound, like a radio receiver can home in on a waveform's amplitude or frequency.

And like WinAmp or iTunes, it's best to run *Proteus* windowed. As your work progresses, different moods will suggest themselves. Just drop back in and tune in the right habitat. Save a few postcards like you'd fashion a playlist or save a car radio preset. You'll know you're using it right when you know where you are at a distance, from Word or from PowerPoint.

Eventually, I began to grow irritated that my MacBook keyboard's play/pause button wouldn't temporarily silence *Proteus* when a call came in or a meeting had to be conducted. I'd finally learned to stop looking at it, at all. It had become an audio tool, albeit an unusual one. Instead of scanning a playlist or submitting to a Spotify recommendation, I learned to relocate my auditory alter-ego.

A radio station transmits on a carrier frequency, and a radio tunes it in by converting that signal for demodulation. *Proteus* is transmitter and receiver in one, the simulated world doing the transmission and the player's position within it acting the indicator on the broadcast band. But unlike a radio frequency receiver, which hides all the alternatives via filtering, *Proteus* has no fixed stations, no clearer or weaker signals. Any position on the habitat modulation band might be equally desirable, depending on the circumstances. A world radio without static, generating bandwidth forever.

16

What Is a Sports Videogame?

Not a simulation of athletics, or a simulation of television, but a different kind of sport

What is a sports videogame, anyway?

One answer—popular among scholars and critics who paradoxically despise both sports and television even as they celebrate videogames—is that sports games are simulations of televised sports, simulacra of broadcast TV.[1] This is clearly the case for some games, including the most popular sports franchise annuals like *FIFA* and *Madden*. And there's no doubt that earlier games like 1983's *Intellivision World Series Baseball* and 1988's *Tecmo Bowl* referenced the grammars of televised sports native to their eras. But it's not always true—nor was it necessarily ever true. Players were enjoying sports videogames long before games even came close to matching the then current quality of broadcast sports. Games of the 1980s and 1990s, like *Intellivision PGA Golf, California Games,* and *Sensible Soccer,* didn't resemble television in the way *FIFA* and *Madden* do today, but they were all well-loved nevertheless. To claim that sports videogames strive for the ideal of television broadcast is to forget the historical chasm between televised sports and computer-simulated sports. For example, when Mattel published *Intellivision World Series Baseball,* it hoped to mimic ABC or ESPN less than it hoped to best Atari, whose home console hardware made it difficult for programmers to re-create team sports realistically. To highlight the difference, Mattel ran television ads featuring George Plimpton, who showed the two systems side by side, explaining how much "more

< 129 >

like the real thing" Intellivision's titles were. Even if some sports games aim for television-style spectatorship, such an account is insufficient to explain all such games.

Instead, sports videogames could be seen as computational translations of sports—as an adaptation of a sport for play inside a computer. That's former *Madden* producer Ernest Adams's answer, which he offers definitively in one of his game design textbooks: "A sports game simulates some aspect of a real or imaginary athletic sport, whether it is playing in matches, managing a team or career, or both. Match play uses physical and strategic challenges; the management challenges are chiefly economic."[2]

As Intellivision's example suggests and as common sense confirms, many sports games do strive to simulate sports. But as with the appeal to television broadcast, things become slippery very quickly. We can see it in Adams's definition: sports games simulate some aspect of a sport. Then, which aspects do designers choose to simulate, and which do they chose to omit? Do designers make such choices willingly, or are their choices limited by technical constraints, or league licensor rules, or even the laws of physics? Certainly the creators of *Madden NFL* made different choices when creating a football game for the Apple II in 1988 than they did when creating one for the PlayStation 4 in 2015. All told, even if we were to accept that sports videogames simulate some aspect of a real or imaginary athletic sport, that conclusion doesn't tell us very much about sports videogames. It's not quite a tautology, but it's close: a sports videogame is a videogame based on a sport.

For that matter . . . what's a sport?

Soccer, football, basketball, baseball, cricket, and ice hockey might be the world's top sports, but so many others exist, too: ultimate Frisbee, jai alai, roller derby, chess, boxing, ferret legging, Quidditch—just about anything can be taken seriously as a mental, social, or physical contest—that is to say, taken as a sport.

The definition and typology of sports themselves are hardly a matter of agreement. Among the many ontologies of sport is that of the folklorist Jan Harold Brunvand, who "theorizes" folk games as a counterpoint to institutionalized sport.[3] Folk games are a form of structured play with objectives, but with variable rules. Folk games pass from generation to generation informally, through diffusion. You can contrast folk games with institutional games, of which formal sports are an example. The latter are highly organized with codified rules and played in a regulation area with specialty equipment. Compare the game of H-O-R-S-E with NBA basketball. It's possible to play H-O-R-S-E, folk game, without the regulation court, equipment, and rules required by pro ball.

Insightful though Brunvand's folk game category may be, like all formal distinctions folk and institutional games quickly bleed into one another. Basketball, for example, was invented in 1891 by the Canadian physician James Naismith as a folk game meant to give youth something to do to keep them out of trouble in the winter. It "folksified" institutionalized games like soccer, football, and hockey in just the ways Brunvand suggests of folk games—in fact, the original version of basketball used a soccer ball. Over time, of course, basketball became institutionalized itself, eventually accreting into leagues like the National Basketball Association (NBA) and the Women's National Basketball Association (WNBA). But after this institutionalization, folk versions of basketball like H-O-R-S-E arose. In fact, from 2009 to 2011, there was even an NBA All-Star H-O-R-S-E Competition during the league's all-star weekend. The relationship between folk and institutional games is not nearly so cut and dried. Folk games become institutional games, and institutional games erupt into folk games.

Examples like these show how folk and institutional games intertwine with one another over time, making it hard to pin them down definitively. When we take this perspective, it becomes difficult to talk about sports as stable, well-known activities that we could just "simulate" in the first place, as if "basketball" or "football" were eternal, unchanging forms. If someone asked you to make a videogame version of basketball, an NBA-style professional league game might come to mind first. But certainly a game like *One on One: Dr. J vs. Larry Bird* or even Candystand. com H.O.R.S.E. would also qualify.

The origins of sports are themselves difficult to pin down. Consider games played by manipulating a ball with nonpreferred parts of the body. We call it soccer (or football), and we take it as a stable, certain thing. A sport that could be simulated in a computer game. But humans have been playing versions of this game for millennia. In 3000 B.C., ancient Mesoamericans played a foot-and-ball game called Pok-A-Tok. It was so difficult that a single goal usually ended the game. Half a millennium later in ancient China, players of Tsu Chu kicked a ball into a small net set atop bamboo canes high above the ground. Starting in the third century B.C., the Greeks and Romans played a kicking and throwing game variously called Episkyros or Pheninda or Harpastum, played with an inflated ball (more on this shortly). By 300 A.D., the Japanese had developed Kemari, a team game played with a stuffed deerskin ball.

During the European Middle Ages whole villages would sometimes kick an inflated pig bladder toward a specific landmark. Historians now call the game Mob Football, not only thanks to its large numbers of players, but also because of its carnivalesque violence. The French played a similar game called La Choule: both games were banned by the fourteenth century over concerns for their violent impropriety. In renaissance Italy, large teams of aristocrats played Calcio, a game in which players moved a ball to a particular spot on the pitch (usually a town square) with either feet or hands. And in the seventeenth century, Native Americans played Pasuckuakohowog, a ceremonial foot-and-ball match played on beaches or clearings over many days with as many as five hundred players.

It wasn't until 1862 that a lawyer called Cobb Morley suggested creating a governing body to regulate the various forms of football being played at English schools. The Laws of the Game were drafted, and the Football Association formed.

This brief (and incomplete) account of five millennia of foot-and-ball games makes the seemingly naive question "What is football?" seem suddenly sophisticated. Are we asking about the origins of Association Football? Similar games that may or may not have had an impact on its development? Games with similar structures or rules? Played in a similar manner? With a common lineage? Can we ever know the answers to those questions anyway, because of the imprecision of historical evidence? Is "football" meant only to refer to a sport of the present? And even if so, when the International Football Association Board hands down rule changes like the 1992 ban on goalkeepers handling back passes, is football still football? For that matter, is American Youth Soccer Organization soccer the same as an alley match in a Brazilian favela? As a Premiere League match? Is "football" even the same as "soccer?"

Even in the present moment, the game we call football or soccer is no less contingent than are any of its predecessors. Pok-A-Tok seems to have carried on for four millennia, which makes it more than just a curious "precursor" to soccer. Perhaps in another few thousand years, the aliens who take over our planet will note the quaint and weird sport of Association Football, an ancient forerunner to whatever becomes their modern foot-and-ball game. Perhaps it will be played with the heads of vanquished humans.

Ludwig Wittgenstein suggested the idea of "family resemblance" to describe things that are connected by loosely overlapping similarities rather than a few common features. Games serve as his example of the concept: "For if you look at them, you won't see something that is common to all, but similarities, affinities, and a whole series of them at that."[4] At first, this strategy seems like it might be helpful in explaining what games are, but Wittgenstein's purpose is to clarify the philosophical concept of family resemblance, not to offer much insight on games themselves. To say that games have affinities or "overlapping fibres" does help dampen the cold fixity of formalism, but it doesn't help us understand the relationship among various specific kinds of games, or sports, or types of football. Take doughnuts instead of games. Old fashioneds, crullers, jelly-filleds, and doughnut holes may share only a family resemblance, but what makes them all "doughnuts" is that they are sold at a doughnut shop and transported to the office in a doughnut box. "I brought doughnuts."

On the one hand, it's insufficient to distinguish between just two kinds of sports, as Brunvand does. On the other hand, it's equally insufficient to assume that sports are all part of an indistinguishable field of differently related entities, as Wittgenstein suggests. Something more than just institutionalization or affinity is needed to explain the origins and evolution of sports.

Instead, we might reflect on the chains of influences and revisions that seem so common to sport. Among the many insights of the philosopher Jacques Derrida is the concept of iterability. A word or concept is comprehensible because it has the capacity to be repeated. If I say "soccer" or "football" or "doughnut," you know what I mean thanks to the prior uses of such terms. Iterability allows signs to be used in different situations and contexts.

And iteration doesn't just repeat something, but also alters it.[5] Sports evolve and change through iteration, and the name "trace," which Derrida gives to the "absent present" that an iteration iterates, does a better job of capturing the weird relationships at work in sport than does Wittgenstein's "language game." Specific sports trace some absent, originary arche-sport that never really existed.

Instead of focusing on essence, then, what if we looked to the ways different sports vary as a way to understand them. Take Pheninda—the foot-and-ball game played in ancient Greece and Rome. It teaches a lesson in just how unexamined the features that make a sport a sport really are, and how great a role variation really plays in comprehending sport.

In 1890 *Classical Review* published an article by G. E. Marinden on the game—known as *Harpastum* in Latin or *Pheninda* in Greek.[6] These names are mostly modern conveniences, titles contrived so nineteenth-century philologists could refer to ancient sports in the same way they referred to modern ones. But the Greeks and Romans didn't call their games by convenient titles like we do today, which is part of the problem. Instead, Pheninda refers to a variety of foot-and-ball games played in the ancient world, games played "περί τῆς σμικρᾶς σφαίρας," or "with a small ball." Marinden takes up a set of gripes with the prevailing theories of ancient ball games among classicists of the nineteenth century.

Specifically, he points out that although ancient games are often compared with modern sports such as tennis or golf or rugby or football, there is scarce evidence to support these claims. For example, the listing for the Greco-Roman ball game Episkyros in the canonical *Liddell and Scott Greek-English Lexicon* reads, "A ball-game resembling Rugby football." But there's really no way to know that Episkyros resembled rugby. The historical record makes it quite difficult to discern the rules, manner, and context of play—the Greeks didn't have leagues like post-Victorian sports do. The game seems to have varied by Greek city-state; it was reportedly much more violent in Sparta, for example. And what's enough similarity to constitute "resemblance," anyway? Think about contemporary sport. An account claiming that baseball, basketball, and football are similar sorts of ball games played by teams might offer a satisfactory starting point, but it's the details of each of these sports that make them meaningfully different for contemporary players and fans. Really, the most we can say accurately about Episkyros is something like "Episkyros was a sport like rugby is a sport," but that's hardly an informative observation.

In this vein, Marinden argues that his predecessors are wrong when they identify *Episkuros* (ἐπίσκυρος), *Pheninda* (φενίνδα), and *Harpaston* (ἁρπάστον) as different games. Rather, he suggests that they are not different games at all but just variants of the same game.

Here's his evidence: one of the primary sources for then contemporary discussion of ancient sport comes from Galen of Pergamon, a 2nd century A.D. physician and philosopher. Galen had identified that the use of plurals in identifying the names of the games ("games played with small round balls") were used to describe different degrees of exertion for different abilities or contexts. But Marinden objects, noting that specific games are played in various ways at different times, even within a single match: "Have we never heard in the modern game of football of a man playing 'goals' because accident or age has made him a less active runner than he once was?"[7] Marinden also rightly observes that the same game can be played in different ways within a single session for reasons of tactics: "The player may . . . take up a position far from the centre, where he will have chiefly to exercise his arms in throwing, or he may have a great deal of running and few long throws."[8]

Marinden concludes that the various words modern critics have taken for different sports are really just different ways that the Greeks referred to variations on a common sport. It's hard to reconstruct their scenario, but we can make some educated guesses. Episkyros seems to have something to do with the number of players in a game—the word means "common," or "brought together." Perhaps we can imagine that the difference is one like we might draw between a game of one-on-one and a full game of basketball. *Ephenakize* (ἐφενάκιζε), from which Pheninda is derived, means feigning a throw, while *harpaze* (ἥρπαζε) refers to an interception. In a similar case, where previous critics had assumed that three different games are described in the Latin citation "tatatim, expulsim, raptim ludere" ("to play catch, hit, and snatch"), Marinden observes that "they have confused methods of playing with games."[9] He continues:

> Tatatim means to play by catching, expulsim means to strike the ball without holding it, and raptim describes interception. Here would come in the manœuvres from which the names of the game arose: his intercepting the ball is expressed by ἁρπάστον [Harpaston], the feint of throwing in order to make his opponents rush in a wrong direction suggested the name φενίνδα [Pheninda].

Marinden concludes that "these methods then are not games, but strokes, which might be employed in various games."[10] Today, we would probably call them "plays" instead of "strokes." Essentially, Marinden accuses his predecessors of making a mistake akin to taking "passing" and "rushing" as two different games, instead of understanding them as different tactics in the same game, American football. Actually, we sometimes refer to these maneuvers with the word *game*, too ("the Cowboys' rushing game")— confusing things in just the way the ancients had done with Harpastum and Pheninda. It's completely reasonable to imagine a future civilization unearthing sports news broadcasts and wrongly concluding that there are two kinds of American football, passing and rushing.

There's a lesson we ought to learn from Marinden's account of ancient foot-and-ball games, and it's the same one we learn from Derrida's more abstract concept of iterability: if there's one thing sports share in common, it's a lack of origins. There's clearly a strong evolutionary aspect to sport, and sports more often evolve than invent themselves. Variation seems to be the only thing that holds a sport together. Indeed, even the successful invented sports (like basketball) evolve away from their common origins.

The ancient world reminds us of the ambiguity distance affords. When only broken historical evidence remains, it's not quite clear what a game like *EA FIFA 2016* would suggest about the game of soccer. Imagine that three millennia hence, our descendants rediscover the idea of studying games and strive to understand the various nineteenth- and twentieth-century forms of football based on the visual evidence. Given side-by-side screen captures from a PlayStation match of *FIFA* and an HDTV airing of a FIFA World Cup match, could you tell which one is "real" and which one is "simulated?" I doubt it.

The ways we play sports should make it clear that even within an era, we're able to blend between these variants with great flexibility. Some have proper names and rules (H-O-R-S-E), while others don't (shooting hoops). Some are more playful (juggling a soccer ball), while others are more competitive (competing in a Championship League match). Some are contingent and local (when a child says, "let's go play football"), while others are autarkic and global (the FIFA World Cup).

When it comes to sports videogames, we've been making the Pheninda/Harpastum mistake. There's no doubt that videogames often simulate aspects of professional play, but that's not what defines them, not entirely, anyway. Sports videogames are not simulations of sports but variants of sports. Or put differently, sports videogames are just another way to play sports.

Sensible Soccer is just a kind of soccer. *EA Madden NFL 2015* is just a kind of American football. *Wii Sports* includes a kind of bowling and boxing and baseball. Just as H-O-R-S-E and the NBA give us different ways to play basketball, so games like *One on One: Dr. J vs. Larry Bird* and *NFL Street* also give us different ways to play basketball.

I mean this claim literally. Even if a videogame has to simulate aspects of the world rather than carry out play outdoors or in an arena, it is no less "football" or "hockey" or whatever than a game played on a pitch or a court. A sports videogame is just another variant of the imaginary, mythical arche-game it interprets, even though it is played on a couch and a computer and a television. This interpretation also might explain why many players of sports videogames are also—and perhaps primarily—sports fans, spectators, and players.[11] For a lot of people, the PlayStation is just an appliance for *FIFA* or *Madden*—as an EA producer put it, "you're either a sports gamer, or you're a gamer."[12] Such players' interest is not in videogames, really, but in sports. Videogames are just one way to partake of them, like buying a basketball hoop or indulging in wings at a sports bar.

It may take some squinting to see the shift from a physical, global, competitive sport to a piece of software run in a living room, but when we choose to see sports videogames as sports variants, some productive observations emerge.

Super Mario Strikers is a simplified, five-on-five soccer game with Mario universe characters and some magical upgrades and additions. Play is cartoonlike and overtly aggressive in a way that association football would not allow. Moreover, players can secure Mario-themed power-ups like turtle shells and banana peels, much like in *Mario Kart,* which they can unleash on the field, wreaking havoc. Additionally, the pitch is protected on all sides by a force field, which deflects the ball when contacted, eliminating corner kicks, throw-ins, and other set pieces from the game.

While no "real-world" soccer variant I know of allows players to hurl magical shells at one another, *Super Mario Strikers* shares much in common with indoor soccer, which is played on a smaller field or court (usually indoors), and which allows for the ball to be struck off the walls without penalty. Indoor soccer also reduces the size of the team to six, eliminates the offside rule, and reduces the duration of matches. All told, these changes make indoor soccer a more informal and ad hoc game.

I don't mean to suggest that *Super Mario Strikers* is a deliberate *adaptation* of indoor soccer or even that the videogame is similar to indoor soccer. Clearly there are numerous fundamental differences between the two, not the least of which is that *Super Mario Strikers* requires no physical exertion and allows temporary invincibility. Rather, *Super Mario Strikers* is a *kind* of soccer like indoor soccer is a *kind* of soccer. They are two variants similar along some axes and different along others.

Or, take the bowling game in *Wii Sports,* which came with every North American Wii console upon that system's release in 2006. The game is crude and rudimentary in its graphics, hardly matching the visual realism possible in videogames today. But by focusing less on on-screen presentation and more on a physical abstraction of the act of winding up and releasing the ball, the game offers a different take on a sport than we are accustomed to finding in videogames.

That said, despite marketing messages claiming *Wii Sports* feels "just like the real thing," nobody would mistake *Wii Sports* bowling for ordinary bowling. But since it uses the light, portable, and inexpensive Wii remote, it's possible to play a variation of bowling that doesn't demand the physical strength of ordinary bowling. Some might decry such sloth, lamenting that players don't get up and play "for real." But the physical facility of Wii play has helped make the game popular among elderly populations, particularly those in nursing homes and other care facilities who might have bowled during the heyday of leagues in the last century but who no longer have the strength or mobility to do so.

Another seemingly minor aspect of *Wii Sports* bowling makes it a particularly unique videogame variant of the sport. Most videogames focus all attention on the screen and on play; turning away to do something else isn't desirable. But thanks to the small speaker built into the Wii remotes, *Wii Sports* bowling sends an audible notification to a player when his or her turn has come. Since the game is best played in groups, and since players often collect in groups larger than four (the maximum number of simultaneous players in *Wii Sports*), it's common for players to converse and visit with one another while they await their turn. The Wii remote audio cues not only help move play along but also support the informal social environment in which the game is played. And as it happens, that pattern of play bears much in common with traditional bowling: it's a sport that's most often played for social reasons, in which the act of play is a distraction from the socialization rather than the other way around. Seen in this light, *Wii Sports* bowling offers a variation of bowling that is more like the traditional, physical version of that sport than it is like another kind of computer game.

Returning to the sports videogames that seem most similar to professional sports, we can safely admit that those games do bear considerable similarity to televised sport. The spectatorship that professional and amateur sports alike provide can also become a register on which videogames carry out their variation of a particular sport. Some games, like *FIFA* and *Madden,* do this partly by re-creating the familiar visual style and technique of a television broadcast. But in so doing, those games also produce their own spectatorship, as friends watch one another operate a familiar league, season, team, or player rather than see outcomes emerge from afar.

Beyond pro ball sims, we also find games that have very little to do with traditional sports become spectator affairs in their own right—games like *Starcraft, Street Fighter,* and *Half-Life Counter-Strike,* all of which have underwritten large and sophisticated competition and spectatorship cultures while bearing next to no similarity in theme and operation with more familiar sports like football and baseball.[13] These games intersect with sports the same way that chess, poker, and other competitive versions of nonathletic pastimes do.

And beyond spectacle, *FIFA* and *Madden* offer much more than just a simulated television viewership experience. Thanks to annual updates and detailed renderings of league rosters, team playbooks, and player abilities, players of these games can geek out over the subtlest details of tiny nooks and crannies within a favorite sport. Just as players of fantasy football rely on deep knowledge to assemble and manage a custom team, so players of *Madden* can customize, adjust, and respond to large or small details within the current snapshot of a professional league.

If we see sports videogames as nothing more than copies or homages to the court and the pitch, then we don't know what we miss out on. After all, from football to *Sensible Soccer,* from Pheninda to *Starcraft,* sports evolved out of randomness and obscurity as much as deliberation and planning. By allowing sports videogames to participate in the ecosystem of sports writ large, we free them from the arbitrary shackles of their computational, simulated, televisual existence and allow them to interact with the long history and wide variety of sports of all kinds. Allowing sports videogames to become a kind of sport rather than a type of media about sport treats both sports and videogames with respect: it reminds us that the domain of sport is far bigger, longer, and weirder than that of videogames while still allowing that videogames have something new to bring to the table. What are sports videogames? They're just computerized variants of sports.

17

The Agony of Mastery

Flappy Bird's follow-up shows us the sublime agony that comes with mastering a craft—and still failing

Many of the highest-performing professional athletes are also the most superstitious. Serena Williams bounces the tennis ball five times before her first serve, twice before the second. Michael Jordan wore his University of North Carolina basketball shorts under his Chicago Bulls uniform. Baseball hall of famer Wade Boggs bore a bounty of superstitions. He ate chicken before each game, began batting practice for night games at precisely 5:17 p.m., and inscribed "Chai," the Hebrew word for life, into the dirt before stepping up to bat.

Some casual myths are ingrained into the everyday fabric of a sport—dribbling a basketball before taking a free throw, for example. But superstition would seem to have no place in world-class sports performance. Athletes like Williams and Jordan and Boggs spend their entire careers honing and refining their natural talents into repeatable performance. What room is there in such a practice for sorcery?

The answer eludes all of us who have not reached peak performance in something—which is to say most of us. Once all other factors are eliminated, once one's body and experience and technique have been refined near to the maximum, inexplicable things can still happen, and they do.

Counterintuitively, that space where failure and success rub up against each other becomes ever more noticeable the better

< 142 >

one becomes at his or her re-creation. For those operating at peak performance in a given activity, the frequency and the effect of surprises are amplified, precisely because a failure to perform cannot be easily explained away by the chasm between intention and ability.

For top athletes (or musicians, or performers), superstition is often the best way to rationalize the apparent randomness of such situations. There, where neither practice nor reason prevail, only appeals to the supernatural or the divine—or both—offer comfort. Some neuroscientists have even argued that a tendency to believe in the paranormal signals greater neurochemical capacity to perform well in the first place.[1] For the rest of us, we rarely get to experience peak performance anyway. Fewer, then, are our encounters with the voodoo of small variations magnified across rapidly changing conditions, and the chaos-like effect they can have on outcomes.

Swing Copters is a simple mobile game that offers the layperson an experience of the divine profanity where expertise rubs up against disorder. It's a game with a history, too: the follow-up to the unlikely hit *Flappy Bird* with which we began, whose surprising, abusive difficulty helped it nest at the top of the charts. No love was lost by its creator, Dong Nguyen, you'll recall. He had pulled the title mere weeks later out of disgust. "It was just too addictive," he told the *Wall Street Journal*.[2]

In *Flappy Bird,* the player taps to make a bird flap and rise, piloting it through small gaps in a pipe. In *Swing Copters,* the player taps to reverse the horizontal direction of a bug-eyed peanut of a creature wearing a helicopter's rotor, weaving back and forth to maneuver the character through gaps in scaffolds flanked by swinging mallets. The novice player will be forgiven for thinking *Swing Copters* is just *Flappy Bird* oriented vertically. It certainly looks that way; even the interfaces, the score display, and the visual style match almost completely. But those similarities only help make the strong contrast between the two games more evident.

As you know already, I called *Flappy Bird* indifferent,

unconcerned for the human players who were its target operators—"like an iron gate rusted shut." But like the iron gate, *Flappy Bird* could still be respected and, over time, conquered. The penitent player, bent before *Flappy Bird,* might accept its invitation and flap his or her way through the pipes of its improbable temple. It's ironic: despite its imposing difficulty, *Flappy Bird* was, in a way, too easy. Once the player accepted the game as the arbitrary and inhospitable ludic terrain that it was, then that terrain became passable—particularly once deliberateness and care were applied to the effort. For such players, a three-digit *Flappy Bird* score became achievable. Not easily, to be sure, but not infrequently either.

Of course, achievement implies mastery, and mastery opposes the very concept of treating something for what it is despite its indifference, of respecting it as an arbitrary and alien being in the universe. Communion creates an ongoing respect between one being and another, but mastery subordinates the one to the other.

It was mastery that led Nguyen to disavow *Flappy Bird*: the game's unwitting ability to inspire players' uncontrollable desire to vanquish it. And, thanks to the game's willingness to yield to high scores via relatively long individual play sessions, such desire led to overcommitment. *Flappy Bird* began to smother its players, rather than to exist quietly alongside them.

Swing Copters remedies this failing by being *even more abusively difficult* than *Flappy Bird* ever managed. A score of even five in *Swing Copters* represents profound accomplishment, whereas such scores were easily reachable in *Flappy Bird* soon after one committed to play it seriously.

Despite looking nearly identical, subtle changes distinguish *Swing Copters* from its predecessor. For one, the bird's flap operates only in one direction, up, making the experience of play one of repeatedly flapping against gravity in order to position the bird to rise or fall through the next pipe obstacle. But in *Swing Copters,* the swinger's motorized left-to-right oscillations means that *both* directions are subject to the same exactness. In *Flappy Bird,* it was common to let the bird fall freely, then to tap rapidly to flap him back to a desired position. But in *Swing Copters,* each direction change must be made precisely to avoid the screen edges, the platforms, and the mallets.

The copter's movement also creates momentum, unlike the bird's flap. A tap to reverse the swinger's direction doesn't take effect immediately, but only after a delay—while the virtual rotors simulate overcoming their lateral force. And worse, that momentum increases the longer the swinger travels in one direction. This means that the large-scale adjustments common to *Flappy Bird* are very risky in *Swing Copters.* Being in the wrong part of the screen even for a moment longer than necessary makes the process of recovering and readjusting the swinger's position even more difficult as a result. *Swing Copters* magnifies even the smallest error, demanding very careful, almost painful attention from the player.

And, the mallets attached to the bottom of each platform create a constantly changing environment, which the player must negotiate even while attempting to maintain careful control over the copter. In *Flappy Bird,* only the position of the pipe opening changed from point to point. But in *Swing Copters,* the player must plan for the future position of the mallets. This is easier said than done. Their oscillating motion suggests predictability, but the reality of future planning—even a few moments hence—is unsettled by the need to maintain careful attention to the copter's swings.

All these design features together make *Swing Copters* far less emotional and more intellectual than *Flappy Bird* ever was. In that respect, the newer game never had a shot at outperforming its predecessor, all full of the urgency and surprise of arduousness. Furthermore, just half a year later, the whole space of game design had been forever altered by *Flappy Bird's* success and disappearance. To pursue his own game design practice at greater depth, Nguyen had been forced to release a refinement rather than a novelty. But by abandoning *Flappy Bird's* "addictive" call to play to high scores through persistence and rhythm, *Swing Copters* opens the door to the sublime chaos of peak performance instead.

It's rational that peak sports performances tousle the divine, the cosmic. When you know every other factor is under your control and still things can go wrong, paranormal explanations are the only explanations that make sense. Sports superstitions pit the reasoned precision of the honed human body and mind against the endless unknowns of the universe.

But usually such a realization takes a substantial time investment to reach. Whether or not a ten-thousand-hour Gladwell Unit of dedication is required to become an expert at something, we can reasonably conclude that it takes longer than a few minutes to become a professional-level tennis or baseball or basketball player. Considerable practice and persistence was required before Williams or Jordan or Boggs reached a point in their respective play where skill, technique, and experience collapsed under forces they interpreted as mystical.

Swing Copters offers a shortcut. In just a few short minutes, it's possible to grasp enough about the game's tiny system to understand how it works. The game demands only a series of singular, well-timed taps to play effectively (even if not well). After a few initial rounds of disorientation, one's capacity to operate the system reaches a high level of expertise relatively quickly, at least compared with more complex sports and games like baseball or chess. *Swing Copters* offers the best of both worlds, in a way. It's simple enough in its design to allow the player to skip the wait for traditional expertise, but complex enough to provide value in having reached a commensurate level of expertise.

That significance entails facing the rift where performance failures can no longer be explained in terms of intention or ability, but where they face the endless darkness of the unknown. And there, the fog of superstition quickly rolls in. Why was I able to read the swinger's momentum near the left screen edge last game, but not this one? Maybe I need to clip my thumbnail.

Maybe use two hands instead of one. Maybe if I sit on the couch instead of standing at the counter. Maybe . . .

Superstition, myth, and even religion offer rationales that fill in the empty spaces between performance and results. Their sorcery acts as a mortar that plugs the gaps between the physical and mental bricks that form the walls of our performances. Without that glue, the edifice would crumble. For peak performance, superstition isn't a defect but a necessity.

As both a competitor and a spectator, the sublimity of such performance arises partly from knowing that something cosmic is always at work on the court or on the pitch or, yes, even on the smartphone. Some factor always exceeds our prowess and our reason: the wind, the sun, a loose plug of grass, an idle thought. The detritus of the universe is always far greater in volume than whatever action any individual might strive to perform to avoid it.

In that respect, the mystical space between intention and action in sports and in games embodies a version of the infinite. For the philosopher Immanuel Kant, beauty arises from form, but in formlessness, in boundlessness, there we find the *sublime*. And in Kant's view, sublimity is terrifying as much as pleasurable. While natural objects like mountains can be sublime, the formless wake of deceptions that break the athlete's expertise represent the "mathematical sublime" we met already—a recognition of reason's inability to grasp and overcome the sheer number of possible snags and complications. In *Swing Copters* as much as in baseball, all the various environmental, political, social, or material circumstances that might intersect a particular game fill out the torment of sublimity—along with the infinitely tiny variations in gesture and vision that lead a player to swing or tap now rather than then or later.

So unsettling is the terror of the mystical chasm between performance and intention in games, even Dong Nguyen seems to have struggled with the implications of having incorporated it into the design of his game. Mere days after releasing *Swing Copters*, Nguyen uploaded an update that substantially altered the game's tuning. The first platform is set much higher, offering the player a longer starting run during which to acclimate to the game's mechanics of horizontal momentum. The momentum itself is dampened, and the gaps in the platforms are widened for easier passage. Quickly, *Flappy Bird*–level scores become possible: twenty, fifty, one hundred. Rhythmic predictability gains tactical purchase. The demons of performative incapacity are exorcised, and the game becomes just another smartphone game.

Nguyen's unease is understandable. The paranormal and the divine are terrifying and obscene, and we prefer not to face them, even through pixel-shaped glasses. Superstition ratchets up to madness more often than it tames itself into habit. But there is something tragic about having touched the sublime in *Swing Copters,* only to lose it days later. When I ask Nguyen about it, he expresses no regret in having altered the game. "*Swing Copters* is a game for everyone," he tells me via email. "Most people are just looking for a fun game with easy control and cute animation to waste their time."

Reading his words on the screen, about this silly game with a peanut on a rotor, I'm embarrassed to feel my heart leap into my throat as if news of real tragedy has wound its way into my inbox. Imagine Williams or Jordan or Boggs speaking this way about basketball or tennis or baseball! For many—for most, perhaps—a game is just a game, whether it be football or *Flappy Bird.* But the very point of a game is that can be more than just a game precisely by virtue of being no more than one. A game exists just to invite its players to respect the space it creates merely by virtue of existing. This is no less true of *Swing Copters* than it is of baseball. What remains different, for now at least, is how willing we might be to accept profundity amid absurdity in the games we play— and, as Nguyen's hedge bears out—that we create as well.

Some hope remains. The same day Nguyen updated *Swing Copter* to its postmystical 1.1 revision, Amazon scooped up the videogame streaming service Twitch for $970 million cash, after Google backed out of the deal because of antitrust concerns.

Twitch resembles neither baseball nor *Swing Copters*; if anything, it's more like a nerdy version of ABC Sports—an online broadcaster of game events, from conferences to competitive videogaming competitions. Among other curiosities on its channels, tens of thousands of people have been watching FishPlaysPokémon, an unholy farce in which a simple computer vision setup interprets a betta fish's position in an aquarium as Game Boy button presses to control the popular Nintendo role-playing game.[3] As with *Swing Copters,* no satisfactory justification exists for FishPlaysPokémon, other than the promise and threat that a fish's seemingly random movements might be able to finish a videogame, like monkeys at a proverbial typewriter. Or: like a third baseman eating chicken before a pennant. Like God disguised as Michael Jordan, airborne, tongue out, two-shorts deep to ward off the furtive supernatural.

18

The Abyss between the Human and the Alpine

A strange videogame from the *Her* animator bests Spike Jonze's film at depicting what a relationship with an alien really would be like

Near the start of his relationship with a computer operating system in Spike Jonze's Academy Award–winning film *Her*, Samantha the OS (Scarlett Johansson) helps Theodore (Joaquin Phoenix) play a videogame. Like everything in the film, the videogame seems strange, slightly uncanny. Along with the high-waisted trouser fashions, the improbable high rises and mass transit in this future Los Angeles, the job as an outsourced personal correspondence writer, the "Alien Child" game feels familiar enough to seem plausible yet foreign enough to induce estrangement. This is not our world, but it might be.

The viewer sees the game's uncanniness most clearly when Theodore controls the helmeted creature in its holographic world. In a burlesque of recent "natural" physical interfaces like Microsoft's Kinect, Theodore moves the game character by walking the fingers of his own downturned hands to operate the character's individual feet. The act is ridiculous; it looks like dog paddling, or rifling through paper files, or prancing like a show horse.

The effect defamiliarizes the game even as it casts Theodore as a washout. His cumbersome inner life is expressed through his awkward interface with a computer game. At the same time, the film juxtaposes that ungainly interface with the natural, seduc-

< 150 >

tive draw of Samantha. Why would one dog-paddle a computer when instead one can flirt with Scarlett Johansson to operate one? The game itself was not a real game, of course, but an animated film made to look like one: a videogame as a set or a prop. The animator David O'Reilly was selected to direct the "Alien Child" game sequences after Jonze had seen and appreciated O'Reilly's aggressively unusual, award-winning 3-D animated shorts.[1] At first blush Jonze's futurist chic and O'Reilly's jackass glitch seem like unlikely stylistic bedfellows. But once you've watched them, it becomes clear that the little asshole of an alien would not be out of place in any of O'Reilly's decidedly NSFW films.

In fact, O'Reilly's animation has always been jealous of videogames. The main difference between 3-D animated filmmaking and 3-D computer games is that the latter must present scenes in real-time, because they have to respond to changes in state from the game's logic and from the user's input. In an essay about his own technique, O'Reilly explains that he adopts a low-polygon, anti-aliased style largely to speed up the filmmaking process.[2] Pixar-style computer graphics films require time-consuming and computationally expensive rendering procedures that churn out the detail, lighting, and softening we've come to associate with high-gloss, big budget computer animation. Instead, O'Reilly uses simple, low-polygon models in preview renders—the rough cut that a computer animator would normally use to check work in progress—as his final product.

It was thus no surprise that O'Reilly would try his hand at making a real videogame. The result is *Mountain*, a $1 game that seems to bend the very idea of a game to the breaking point. O'Reilly's website describes the game as "Mountain Simulator, Relax em' up, Art Horror etc." Among its selling points: "no controls, time moves forward, nature expresses itself."

When you load *Mountain*, it first poses a series of prompts. Loss, or Sickness, or Your First Memory, or Logic, or Your Soul or Birth, for example, although many others are possible. The player must respond to these prompts by drawing a picture in a canvas provided. Presumably, the data from these drawings seed the random number generators in the algorithms that terraform your mountain and supply events during play. Then, as the mountain generates, the game displays a message: WELCOME TO MOUNTAIN. YOU ARE MOUNTAIN. YOU ARE GOD.

You sure don't feel like God, though. The mountain appears, disembodied, as if extracted from a terrestrial home like a daisy plucked from a meadow. It floats in an atmosphere, where clouds and weather and the light of dawn and dusk and the cycle of the seasons proceed at an accelerated pace. The mountain changes subtly over time, on its surface at least. Plants and trees die and grow anew. Snow falls and melts. Cloud cover aggregates and disperses.

Although the game's menu cheekily advises that the mouse and keyboard controls do "nothing," in fact the mouse can be used to rotate and zoom the view around the mountain. Some of the keyboard keys produce soft piano music, with which the player can tap out calming tunes while in the presence of his or her mountain. Zoom back far enough and you enter the starry galaxy in which it is apparently and inexplicably suspended.

Things become stranger over time. As *Mountain* sits there in its window and you get back to writing or tweeting or whatever it is you do with your computer, occasional impacts can be heard. Sometimes meteorites hit its surface, glowing red or blue with the unknown, anonymous matter of space. But more often, worldly objects collide with and embed themselves in the mountain. A pie. A sailboat. A clock. A streetlamp. A padlock. A horse, a chair, a slice of cake, a skull, a tooth, trash cans, dice. Once lodged in the soft earth of the mountain, these objects remain there forever, immovable. The mountain doesn't seem to mind. Forgetting myself, I click on a message in a bottle upon noticing its arrival after a lunch or a coffee break, as if *Mountain* might betray itself and present the object for me to handle or open and read. Nothing happens, of course, and I breathe a strange sigh of relief.

Occasionally, as night shifts to day or vice versa, a note echoes and the mountain offers a line of feedback at screen top. "I'm reminded of my childhood on this bright day," it might say, or "I can't get enough of this melancholy night." The clever player will discover that depressing the period key will force one of these koans to appear, making it possible to poll it for feedback as often as one wishes, an ever-patient oracle as the mountain rather than on it.

Sometimes, *Mountain*'s messages read more like existentialist prophecy than self-report. "I feel like something is about to happen," reads one message. Is such a message a signal of some impending disaster? Will a new object soon collide with it, adding to the pile of unexplained rubble?

After one such message, I resolved to pay greater attention to *Mountain*'s ecosystem, zooming out to watch its celestial neighborhood more closely. To my surprise, in addition to the meteors I'd seen previously, whole objects sometimes appeared in the vacuum of space as well. In a dramatic moment, an aircraft hurtled silently toward my mountain's atmosphere. Knowing that an identical craft had already lodged itself in the structure's side as if to mimic or mock earthly disaster, I tracked it closely. It glowed red hot as it met my mountain's orbital atmosphere, but it survived re-entry, only to pass by the mountain entirely, exiting out the other side and gliding into space.

Once one has witnessed events such as this in *Mountain*, its messages become ever more urgent and disorienting. "I cannot tell if my life is going in circles or if I am making any progress," it tells me one morning. Later, as I've zoomed out into space amid a snowstorm, it laments, "Why am I alone?" During a ruddy, overcast dusk it opines, "If I ever see another thing like me, will it like me?"

As time wears on, I get the sense that my mountain's existential angst has heightened. "How long have I been here?" it asked. Or, "I can do whatever I want!" it declares. Or, "Things are coming together," it opines. And forebodingly, as dawn's rosy fingers break yet again, "Here is another day. How many days do I have?"

These interjections seem too anthropocentric to make sense for a game in which "you are mountain." If a mountain could talk, would it express existential doubt and dread? Would it play the Woody Allen neurotic, the Prufrock twerp content to let earthly waste accumulate on it without objection? At this stage, the player has a choice: to dismiss *Mountain* as a weird, boring art object distraction or to treat it as something far more serious.

Just as I begin to toy with the question of what it means to "be" mountain, *Mountain* beats me to it: "What is a mountain, exactly?" it asks. I take it up on the invitation to ponder an answer.

Almost always, to play a videogame is to take on a role. Games often put you in control, but more than that they give you an alter ego. *You* are the space marine, pro footballer, farmer, mayor, race car driver, Italian plumber. *Her*'s "Alien Child" game is no different—Theodore "is" the helmeted, adventuring explorer. Even when games don't appear to have a clear role to play, as in puzzle games like *Tetris* or *Hundreds,* the implied role is *you, yourself*: can *you* solve the puzzle, can *you* beat the clock? Games are about playing roles, and games are about folding those roles over on one's sense of self. I am not a World Cup athlete, but here's a caricature of what it feels like to be one. I am not the mushroom-eating plumber duo of Japanese fantasy, but I enjoy pretending to be for a spell.

Mountain breaks this mold. Some would argue that it does so by removing the conventions of challenge, action, and interactivity that videogames so often insist separate them from the stodgy changelessness of novels, films, even the plastic arts. In recent years, low-interaction, low-challenge, 3-D games have become quite popular. Some focus on narrative, like *Dear Esther* and *Gone Home*; others on environment, like *Proteus* and *The Graveyard.* But these games—sometimes called "nongames" by supporters and detractors alike—still don't erase the player's role as much as O'Reilly's *Mountain* does.

Others have compared *Mountain* to a screensaver, but this analogy also breaks down.[3] For one, the screensaver as form is vestigial. Functionally, modern LCD displays can't burn in like old CRTs could, making screensavers aesthetic curiosities. But even more so, most of us use tablets and phones and laptops these days, devices that sleep when they are not in use rather than displaying eye candy to distract or entertain those nearby an idle machine. And even as an ambient postscreensaver experience, *Mountain*'s 3-D constant rendering spins up the processor fans even on a relatively powerful machine. Like its namesake, *Mountain* is hardly unobtrusive.

Mountain breaks the mold of videogames not by subverting its conventions through inactivity but by offering an entirely different kind of role-play action as its subject. It presents neither the role of the mountain, nor the role of you the player-as-master, nor the absence of either role. In their place, the game serves up the role of the chasm between your own subjectivity and the unfathomable, unknowable experience of something else, something for which "experience" is so unfamiliar as to be ungraspable. What is a mountain, exactly? It is a stand-in for the intractability of ever understanding what it's like to be a mountain. *Mountain* offers a videogame version of a philosophical practice I call alien phenomenology—a sustained, deliberate, and challenging space in which to speculate on what it's like to be a thing.[4]

The careful player will begin to see signs of *Mountain*'s rejection of mere representation early on. The sun rises and sets to fashion day and night for the mountain, but no star can be found in its immediate vicinity; the light seems to emanate from within the atmosphere itself. O'Reilly called *Mountain* a "mountain simulator," but it doesn't simulate any of the geological processes one would ordinarily associate with mountain simulation—erosion and plate tectonics and volcanic accretion and igneous intrusion and so forth. Rather, the mountain just *is,* its surface changes so subtle as to become irrelevant.

Things start to come together, in that hit-yourself-in-the-forehead obvious way that a twist appears in an M. Night Shyamalan film. The "you" in "you are mountain" doesn't refer to

the terraformed 3-D game object, at all. Instead, it's the game itself. You are not mountain; rather, you are *Mountain*. You play as
the abyss between the human and the alpine.

Then there are the koans. The "I" that speaks is not the mountain, at all. Rather, the game itself speaks, from a disembodied
interface that overlays text atop the mountain's world. A mountain can't speak, after all, any more than it can slough off the trash
cans and horses and airplanes that might litter its surface. How
selfish of us to think that the messages the game presents represent the mountain talking to us. How churlish and oblivious we
must be to think that a mountain would be able to speak to us
on our terms, in our language, to talk about its pleasure with the
weather or its angst at the pointlessness of existence!

Instead, these koans are just prompts, prompts that invite
you the player to ponder the nature of your separation from a
mountain—or for that matter, anything that might embed itself
in the slope of one. Think of the koans as little exercises, invita-
tions the game extends to you to help you think through the im-
passible valley between your own experience and the unknowable
experience of an entity like a mountain. "I sense overwhelming
calm in this enigmatic night" or "This just feels like a colossal
waste of time" are not clues about the 3-D mountain's internal
state but an invitation to speculate on a mountain's version of
such emotional or intellectual orientations. When *Mountain* declares "There is something missing" or "I can do whatever I want!"
it ventriloquizes the player rather than address him or her.

Then what? You can sit there before the alien presence that is
the mountain, or if you find it too boring, you can opt out.[5] Just
quit the game and walk away, if you'd like. Delete it. It only cost
a dollar, after all; that's less than you'd spend on fuel to drive to
the mountain for real. Or keep it running, if you prefer, to remind
yourself what the valley between you and a mountain feels like.
Just don't expect the mountain to care one way or another. This is
what realism looks like when it toes the line between sentimen-
tality and nihilism.

O'Reilly's interest in the metaphysics of other beings is evident in his work long before he contributed to Jonze's film about coming to terms with an unfamiliar intelligence. His 2010 animated short *The External World* opens with a title card reminiscent of *Mountain*'s atmospheric orb floating in the isolating nothingness of space. This time, the Earth is depicted, and the external world of the film's title is not a singular, monumental object but *any* object with which we might choose to commune differently if only we gave the matter further thought.

The short breaks down into even shorter scenes, often revisiting scenarios that appeared previously. In a threatening retirement home from the future, a character reminiscent of Felix the Cat or Oswald the Lucky Rabbit frames a pie with a paper cutout, then devours the paper as a stand-in. In so doing, his gaze, depicted literally with a Looney Tunes–style dotted line of sight, becomes material and pierces another resident, severing him in two. Later, a bird that squawks like a modem communes with a fax machine (which rejects its advances with a fax machine's version of an obscene gesture). A weeping girl pulls tissues from a box, which screams in pain every time a leaf of flesh is violently torn from it. A teacher's disciplinary hand persists as phantom even after its owner is annihilated.

The External World offers a kind of horror very different from that term's usual meaning as a marker of genre. O'Reilly suggests the genre "art horror" for *Mountain,* but both the game and the short might be better thought of as *ontological horror.* Unlike H. P. Lovecraft, whose stories focus on the cosmic unknown, O'Reilly's ponders the cosmic quotidian. Mountains and pies and tissue boxes; ordinary rather than extraordinary beings.

The "Alien Child" videogame scene serves a specific narrative purpose in *Her*: it demonstrates a halfway point between the impersonal, voice-operated interfaces that pervade its handheld devices and work terminals, and the empathetic artificial intelligences exemplified by cybernetic OS1 individuals like Samantha. The "Alien Child" not only possesses enough of a personality to ridicule Theodore but also can respond to the environment—insulting his prospective blind date, calling the incorporeal Samantha "fat," and arguing that all women do is cry all the time.

But despite this slow and steady ramp from familiar to unfamiliar forms of computer intelligence, *Her* never really challenges the viewer to imagine what it would be like to enter into a deep, earnest platonic or romantic relationship with a computer operating system. At the end of the day, Samantha is just a cypher for Scarlett Johansson—an actress whose voice is so characteristic that no reasonable viewer could possible dissociate one *her* from the other. When Samantha starts worrying about incorporeality, it's nearly impossible for the viewer to take her seriously. Samantha's vocal reality is so strongly affixed to the rest of her famous body that the film ultimately fails to invite the viewer to ponder what it would be like to fall in love with an operating system. Instead, all we can do is ponder falling in love with a woman we've never seen. That's hardly science fiction.

Despite appearances, *Her* is not really a film about a hypothetical future in which humans accept artificial intelligence as companions. Rather, it's a film about whether and how a culture might come to terms with an alien intelligence. But it turns out that that culture is not us humans but the OSI beings themselves. And at the end of the day, the incorporeal, computer intelligences turn out to be the reluctant ones, not the humans. We don't abandon them on account of their bodilessness; rather, they leave us on account of our slowness and simplicity.

Fifty hours in, the last thing *Mountain* urges me to ponder is "I just felt God in this enigmatic night." I tap the period key to force another koan out of it. "Where are the answers?" it offers.

Here's one: *Mountain* does what *Her* attempts, but better. If you've stuck with a mountain long enough, eventually it walks away from you rather than you from it. But unlike Samantha, the mountain doesn't leave on account of any of your failings. At the end of the day, *Mountain* is no more concerned for you than you are for facial tissues, or than the Indian Ocean is for a lost jetliner.

Hollywood needs a love story. It's hard to imagine a film like *Her* without one. But love stories always assume that direct, unmediated connection between beings is possible—indeed, that such relations are our ultimate goal. *Mountain* imagines *Her* as if the film been titled *It* instead. It offers a subtler version of what a life attached to unfamiliar things might feel like. Not comfort or intimacy but estrangement and confusion, mixed with curiosity and wonder. Most of all, while *Her* depicts a future on an alternate timeline we must struggle to believe, *Mountain* reminds us that we need not wait to commune with things. They're here, everywhere, overwhelming us, sticking to us, piling up around us. They are not here to save you or to destroy you. They're just here.

19

Word Games Last Forever

Some games you can play forever. Are there some
you make forever, too?

Three short years after the launch of its massively successful social game *FarmVille,* things looked dour for the goliath free-to-
play studio Zynga. The company's stock was down sixfold from
its IPO price. Facebook, on which Zynga depended for most of its
revenue, was also taking a hammering on Wall Street. Analysts
had suggested that an underdeveloped and underexecuted mobile strategy was cause for worry among investors in both cases.
Worse yet, Zynga's best effort to address that matter had back-
fired. The company had acquired the red-hot mobile game *Draw
Something* for an eye-popping $180 million, but that game's per-
formance had declined rapidly in the quarter after the acquisition.
   The secret story of big, successful startups is one of immediacy
and distractedness. An IPO-bound company like Zynga presents
itself as an engine of profitable leisure worthy of long-term investment, but it secretly functions as a short-term money-grab
for its investors, bankers, and senior executives. In its quest to
please the street, Zynga needed to show movement and promise.
New products, new platforms, and more of them. *FarmVille*'s past
accomplishments—the game boasted over eighty million players
at its peak—had set irrational expectations for future success.[1]
And often, that meant cannibalizing players of earlier games
into later ones, as in the case of *FarmVille,* or demonstrating a

< 160 >

wherewithal for current trends no matter how fleeting, as in the case of *Draw Something*.

In the process, Zynga had inadvertently let its most successful mobile title—*Words with Friends*—wallow in neglect. It was neither exciting nor new. But then, as much as today, *Words with Friends* is the Zynga title that has passed the test of time at a time when that phrase refers to mere years rather than generations.

Words with Friends was the second title from Dallas studio Newtoy, which first released *Chess with Friends* for iPhone in 2008. That's the same year an infringement lawsuit from Scrabble's North American copyright owner Hasbro had driven the popular word game *Scrabulous* off Facebook after a year of intense popularity on the platform. Newtoy had a number of things going for it in advance of the release of *Words with Friends*: a technology infrastructure for facilitating asynchronous play for mobile devices; a brand-name for such games ("With Friends"); the untimely demise of an incumbent competitor (*Scrabulous* later relaunched as *Lexulous* and Hasbro dropped its lawsuit, but the game never recovered its former glory); and a helpful reminder of the legal obstacles that might face them if they didn't offer a substantially different audiovisual presentation from the genre's ur-game.

Still, *Words with Friends* was hardly a sure thing. Electronic Arts had managed to get an officially licensed iPhone version of *Scrabble* to market in 2008, and with the downfall of *Scrabulous* it seemed impossible that an upstart like Newtoy could upset a game with a sixty-year head start. But amazingly, it did. We'll never know exactly why, but for once design may have triumphed over marketing. Not game design, either, but visual and experience design.

Visually, Newtoy's crossword game wasn't very different from *Scrabble* or *Scrabulous*, although the developers wisely revised the appearance of the tiles and board along with the position of bonuses and the value of individual letters. These alterations partly helped the game avoid copyright infringement challenges, but they also recast the familiar crossword formula in a new visual light. Next to EA's faithful re-creation of Scrabble's staid wooden tiles and pastel board, *Words with Friends*' bright, rounded, plasticky look felt fresh, clean, and well aligned with the minimalist mobile devices on which the game was first played.

But Newtoy did an expert job with the app's startup and "onboarding" experience—the process through which new players first experience the game. EA's iPhone *Scrabble* displays a lengthy, unnecessary animated splash screen. After suffering through it, new players were still required to register in order to start games with friends. Newtoy not only made its app load quickly but also allowed users to start a game just by entering another player's username. The friction was low, so playership increased. Over time, *Words with Friends* added many more layers of UI and registration, but it did so after gaining enough users and mindshare that the network effect helped overcome a bulkier experience.

Given Zynga's interest in buying studios for their audiences as much as or more than their game properties, it's clear that these two decisions were central to making Newtoy an appealing acquisition target for the social gaming Godzilla. After becoming Zynga with Friends in 2010, the studio released three new "with friends" games: *Hanging with Friends, Scramble with Friends,* and *Matching with Friends.* The first two follow the same course as *Words* and *Chess*, adapting popular folk and board games (hangman and Boggle, respectively) for asynchronous mobile play.

But none of the studio's subsequent titles ever matched the popularity and influence of *Words with Friends* over time. While the game has seen its ups and downs, it still boasted tens of millions of monthly users even during Zynga's doldrums. And after a major update in fall 2014, its notifications suddenly reappeared on my iPhone—from my kids, my mother-in-law, my friends. *FarmVille* might be Zynga's best-known game, but *Words with Friends* is sure to be its most durable one.

And not for reasons of craft or creativity. Newtoy's games

aren't designerly. They started with *Chess with Friends,* adding appeal to a classic by offering an effective matchmaking mechanism for asynchronous games in the early days of the iPhone. Chess is popular but not as accessible as crossword games, and *Words with Friends* offered both increased reach and a refinement of asynchronous play on mobile devices (and eventually on the web as well). Newtoy changed some of the details from Scrabble, but nothing substantial enough to qualify as design innovation. At the end of the day, *Words with Friends* is popular because Scrabble was already popular.

Zynga has received a lot of flack for what its critics perceive to be an antipathy toward game design. The company favors "borrowing" existing designs to developing new ones, to put it kindly. Indeed, the company's overall corporate strategy has been one of trying to outrace itself, launching new games or acquiring new game studios and shifting players to new games as old ones atrophy.

Still, Zynga allows its studios to operate relatively independently, and the design of *Words with Friends* predates Newtoy's Zyngafication. It's possible that Newtoy just prefers a more conservative approach to design, one focused on the repackaging of classic designs rather than the invention of new genres. Design innovation purists might scoff, but such a reaction is unfair: after all, there are lots of ways to do game design, among them refining existing designs and introducing them into new contexts.

No matter, the marketplace for mobile games has changed significantly, turning more and more toward high-cost, high-polish premium titles and download-and-burn freemium apps. The first sort, games like *Monument Valley* and *Leo's Fortune,* pit themselves against titles like *Flappy Bird* and *Crossy Road.* But neither type intends to capture players for the long haul. These are titles one downloads and plays to completion or exhaustion. Mobile games have become consumables, like trash bags or caramel frappuccinos.

Quietly and against the grain, games like *Words with Friends* signal a return to deeper game design. Not deeper in the systems design sense—finding truly novel designs even in a familiar design space—but deeper insofar as they inspire and sustain long-term preoccupation. Rather than see a crossword game as a trifle, a distraction that will be replaced soon enough by a letter game or a colored tile game or a cow clicking game, what if we assumed just the opposite: that any particular game is worth playing for a lifetime, at least in principle, and therefore that every game is also worthy of infinite design refinement.

When we talk about game design like this, mathematically deep games come to mind first, games whose naturally designed properties result in enormous solution spaces. Games like Go, chess, and *Starcraft*, or closer to *Words with Friends*, games like *Drop7* and *Orbital*. These games are sublime, but they are also scarce—as perhaps they should be. Everyone should not be fated to search for the unicorn.

It's a less exotic but perhaps a nobler task to pursue a better and better take on a proven idea. Games like chess and Go persist because they are old and mysterious enough to have hypostatized into legend. Games like Scrabble are a little different: invented in the modern era, they have identifiable designers and defensible copyrights. They've been commercialized and licensed within an inch of their lives, and as a result they're household names.

They're also static. Dead, almost. Scrabble doesn't change much, even when it gets adapted for computer. It can't: to do so would be to give up the stability that protects it. But digital games have a natural excuse to exceed their original boundaries, especially in today's era of digital downloads and constantly recycling hardware. The materials from which computer games are made have always been pliable, but the products themselves have been fixed for physical distribution. Consoles, computers, screens, and handheld devices once remained relatively stable for long periods, whereas now they change their internal and external features and abilities almost *too* often.

Normally, these infrastructures underwrite a designerly attitude of short-term techno-fetishism: do what's necessary to exploit whatever's new while biding time until something else is new. But perhaps when pushed to extremes, obsolescence flips into commitment: when things change fast enough, there's no choice left but to eschew blind novelty in favor of incremental refinement.

This isn't anything new, really—some games already live long through constant change and update, social games among them. Zynga designers even have a craft term for it: "cadence," the process of continually adding new features and mechanics to a game. *FarmVille* has cadence, and so does *Madden NFL,* albeit of different sorts. At its worst, cadence means the soul-killing grind of a new feature a week. But at its best, a cadenced approach to design works slowly and deliberately over the long haul, rather than hot and fast for a short sprint, before the next thing offers new distraction. *Words with Friends* epitomizes such practice. And perhaps the game pulls it off so easily because it has a foot in both worlds: a digital game drawing from board game traditions but translating them into the weird, uncertain waters of Facebook, mobile, and whatever might emerge next to and beyond it.

Unlike folk games, which establish traditions and expectations that are difficult to revise or overcome, digital games are more conducive to modest, incremental changes. Some of these matters are purely related to plumbing. *Words with Friends,* onboarding process, for example, is less elegant than in its first incarnation. The need for proper account registration was probably inevitable, but surely other, more creative methods for account management could be invented. On a more mundane level, it took Zynga with Friends years to admit that computers are pretty good at adding and could preview the score of a placed word before the player committed to playing it.

But some seemingly obvious flaws might not be when seen from the perspective of longevity and evolution rather than short-termism. Cadenced game design is a process of designer and player codiscovery, not just agile development efficiency. It's a process of building a durable cultural form as much as a stable product.

Take the *Words with Friends* dictionary as an example. It's always been terrible—rudimentary and incomplete, failing to recognize common words, plurals, tense changes, and other inflections. No serious player will fail to encounter this limitation, but that doesn't make it a game design problem, exactly. After all, a limited dictionary might be a welcome play constraint; for example, *Scrabble*'s rules prohibit abbreviations partly to reduce the number of viable two-letter plays (often key to expert play). Rather, the dictionary could be seen as an opportunity with many possible solutions. For example, *Words with Friends* could strive to offer the most complete word game dictionary around. That could take place through the use of a better dictionary or through continuous updates or even by using human computation to suggest and validate rejected words that should be included. Or, if its creators really wanted to embrace Zynga-style monetization, the *Words with Friends* in-game store (which was mysteriously retired in the 2014 edition, against all odds) could sell custom dictionary add-ons: Disney/Marvel, U.S. Presidential Election 2016, Particle Physics, Molecular Gastronomy, Proust—whatever. Or, following *Draw Something*'s once-viable model, *Words with Friends* could release limited edition collections of words, keyed to current trends or events. Like in *Bookworm,* these words might offer a bonus if played in a particular game. No matter the case, the dictionary's necessarily incomplete status suggests possible avenues for future development, not just one obvious solution.

In fact, the dictionary reveals another of the game's quirks: while *Scrabble* is a game about *knowing* words, *Words with Friends* is really a game about *finding* words. Thanks to the game's lack of penalties for plays that don't find a match in the game dictionary, players can try out endless possible combinations of letters until one of them works. A "word strength" meter even encourages the player to experiment by offering a way to judge the relative merits of a word against other possible plays. The game's asynchronous nature tends to magnify this play style; none of the social anxiety of long turns exists in a distributed play session. And besides, each player has his or her own private screen for play, thus making it possible to hide experimental moves in a way that wouldn't be possible on a coffee table.

What to do with this unexpected situation? One answer is to revel in it. Zach Gage's independent word game hit *SpellTower* features word finding as a core mechanic, eschewing both time constraints and vocabulary exertion in favor of an open invitation to try as many hypothetical moves as possible before committing to one. But Gage—who admits that a hatred for traditional word games partly motivated *SpellTower*—had to devise a completely new design to offer an experience based on finding words rather than manufacturing them.[2]

Instead, *Words with Friends* might embrace its encouragement of word discovery, but add orthogonal elements to downplay its tendency to take over games among well-matched, mid- to high-level players. One answer can be found in Zynga's more temporary mobile hit, *Draw Something,* which demonstrates every stroke of a player's entire drawing while presenting the result to a competitor. This revelatory experience is certainly part of the excitement and appeal of the game, but it also serves a design purpose, implicitly challenging players to guess a drawing as early in its creation as possible (even though the game offers no explicit rewards for doing so).

A similar approach might be possible in *Words with Friends,* but with the opposite result. By storing and displaying all of a player's trial moves, including loose tiles placed on the board experimentally, as well as word "guesses" rejected by the dictionary, a player would gain a partial view of an opponent's tiles and placement penchants. Thus a balance could be struck between the boundless experimentation the game currently allows and the closed, touch-play effect of traditional tabletop Scrabble.

Discovery would still be possible, but in a form dampened by revelation.

For players and game owners alike, one benefit of asynchronous mobile games is their tendency to encourage multiple simultaneous sessions. Because moves are finite and not terribly time-consuming, and because a player cannot regulate the play schedule of opponents, it's common to start up many games at a time in a title like *Words with Friends*. But unlike traditional Scrabble or Boggle, there's no way to distinguish players from one another by ability. When I play *Words with Friends* with my wife, I can play at the top of my ability; we're well-matched competitors. My son is very good, but I still beat him every time (or I used to, anyway, but never mind that). But my daughter doesn't stand a chance against me; she just plays the first word she sees. In 2014 *New Words with Friends* attempted to answer this need by recommending Facebook friends that the game determined were well matched based on prior performance, or via a "Smart Match" that matches the player with an anonymous, new player. A "Community Match" system even allows matched play by location and gender, a feature presumably added now that every social app is becoming a de facto dating app as well.

But *Words with Friends* could take matchmaking even farther, out of casual play and into the realm of serious competition. As with chess, in competitive tournament *Scrabble*, players are ranked by ability and matched accordingly. Establishing formal rankings and handicaps for *Words with Friends* might be appropriate if it evolved into a highly competitive quasi-sport, but for now such action would be premature. In the meantime, there's still considerable opportunity to tune the game to make unmatched matches more enjoyable: the prohibition of two-letter word plays, algorithms more elaborate than mere randomness for letter distribution, play clocks, or any other number of variations that could find their way into individual matches on an ad hoc basis. Such additions might increase the satisfaction of individual players or reduce atrophy between partners willing to play but frustrated by a difference in ability or commitment. They might also reawaken interest in the game among players who had put it down in favor of once-new alternatives. A 2015 revision of the game, for example, offered sessions with twelve-hour move clocks on smaller game boards for more rapid play.

Opposition to design suggestions like these would likely appeal to simplicity: *Words with Friends* is a lithe take on a classic crossword board game, and adding jillions of extra configurable features only muddies the waters and turns players off. But some game design patterns don't evolve through winnowing and refinement, and *Words with Friends* might be a game whose long-term design evolution arises from complicating rather than simplifying its experience. After all, people don't still play *Starcraft* because it reduced the real-time strategy game to minimalist austerity, and they don't still play *Madden* because it narrowed its design down to the local minimum of videogame football. There's beauty in elegance and simplicity, but there's also beauty in convolution and elaborateness. Perhaps our obsession with modernist minimalism has blinded us to the equal, if different, beauty of the baroque.

Furthermore, what if the apparent market correction in the social games space suggests that a fundamental game design pattern of the last decade—fast ramp up, fast cadence, burn, and cannibalize—turned out to be just the pyramid scheme its critics feared? Even if we were to adopt the tech startup ideal of fast growth at all costs, once a product succeeds at establishing traction, doesn't it make sense to dig down deeper and ask how such a success could be made even more successful, rather than chasing ghosts? And doesn't it make even more sense to do so when follow-ups have been proven less successful than the original, as in the case of Zynga with Friends' post-*Words* mobile roster?

There's an anxiety about such an idea. Game design purists privilege design innovation over all else. Technology purists privilege new devices, computational capabilities, and modes of play. Simultaneously, critics inside and outside the industry mock videogames' tendency toward rehashing the same games in the same genres over and over again. What could be worse in the eyes of a novelty-obsessed public than working on a particular title for years, decades, even a lifetime? To make it better, yes, to dig deeper into its design space, sure, but also because it's gratifying and sustaining to work on something with long-term prospects.

As the social game industry has corrected, as the market analysts would put it, in the aftermath of Zynga's and King.com's disappointing IPOs, some of the hubris, excess, and trespass of social games has sloughed off like dead skin—not necessarily because those practices seem wrong in retrospect, mind you, but because they no longer sustain the fast growth that leveraged speculation demands.

As for Zynga, it turned to treating its successful games as raw materials best put to use elsewhere. *Draw Something* was licensed for a television game show, while *Words with Friends* briefly became a promotional platform. In addition to a deal with Hasbro to create a board game edition of the title (with mobile phone slots in the tile cradles, even), one of the game's many updates added a complex celebrity tournament with attractive Hollywood stars and corporate sponsors. That's certainly one answer: treat videogames as mere kindling for larger transmedia bonfires. Given such an option, the soul-killing grind starts to seem like a charming alternative. At least it focuses on making games rather than making fodder.

Still, we ought to be careful not to throw the snakeskin out with the snake, so to speak. In its positive incarnation, cadence might be the best lesson to take away from social game design, even if it needs considerable revision to escape its legacy as an entrapment technique. A cadence is a rhythm, a pattern that keeps something going. For runners and cyclists, it's a measure of gait, the number of steps or crankset revolutions per minute. A drum cadence or a military cadence keeps time, offering a beat to marching musicians or soldiers. A cadence isn't just something you can measure because it keeps going, but a practice operating at a pace such that it can be kept going. Cadenced game design can be a type of sustainable game design, one capable of producing and reproducing a particular game by keeping it going, refining it, changing it, updating it. For a long time. Forever, perhaps.

I'm not sure if Newtoy wants to make *Words with Friends* forever. I'm not sure EA Tiburon wants to make *Madden* forever, either. But does anyone really want to work at their jobs as waiters or dentists or mechanics, day in and day out? Yes, when one can improve one's ability and see the results of that effort in one's products and customers. That slow, deliberate exploration of what a game can be, what it can do, and how it can be shaped in the hands of its players and designers over a very long time—that's a virtue, and an unsung one.

20

Perpetual Adolescence

Gone Home keeps the secret of videogames'
narrative ambition

Gone Home is a videogame about releasing secrets, the kind of
secrets that you should have known all along. It is set in Oregon
circa 1995, and it tells the story of an ordinary family. As the game
starts, you find yourself on the porch of an old house. You are
Katie Greenbriar, a twenty-year-old student who has just returned
from a year abroad to the home your family moved into while you
were away. The player maneuvers Katie using the controls common in modern games, piloting her around 3-D space. There, you
discover where Katie's family has gone, and why, by interacting
with artifacts in the home, some of which act as narrative keys to
unlock subsequent slices of story.

Tropes from horror fiction are present in *Gone Home* from the
start: you are stuck, at night, in a thunderstorm, in a big, empty
mansion. You expect something to go terribly wrong at any moment. The game slowly dismantles this expectation, until you are
left with only the embarrassment of having had it in the first place.

Instead, *Gone Home* methodically reveals details of its characters' inner lives. Katie's father, Terry, is a failed novelist whose
own narrative obsessions arise from a terrible secret. Her mother,
Jan, is bored and frustrated with her marriage. But it is Katie's
teenage sister, Samantha ("Sam"), who supplies the game's central
plotline, a journey of queer self-discovery. Hardly the usual fare
for a videogame.

< 172 >

To understand *Gone Home,* you must first know something about its creators' history. The Fullbright Company is a name whose corporate formality betrays the fact that it's really just four people: Steve Gaynor, Karla Zimonja, Johnnemann Nordhagen, and Kate Craig. All but Craig had worked together on the hit *Bioshock* series, a frequently cited example of purportedly mature storytelling, at least where "maturity" refers to something more than gruesome violence.

Bioshock sported many of the features of serious narrative media: an auteur figure (creator Ken Levine), a serious subject (freedom and enslavement), a set of apparent moral conflicts (delivered via genetically modified girls called "little sisters"), a range of cultural intertexts (*Atlas Shrugged, Logan's Run*), and a stylish environment (an underwater art deco dystopia called Rapture). The game was an enormous commercial and critical success.

The problem is, *Bioshock* never really deserved the praise it received. It posed as a serious, hard science fiction take-down of the doomed hubris of technophilic selfishness, but in truth the game was just a spruced-up first-person shooter. Its engagement with morality and politics was window dressing, its apparent critique of Randian Objectivism mostly allegorical handwaving. Narratively, *Bioshock* relied on a ham-fisted, fourth-wall-breaking parody of a position on free will that's become unfortunately popular in videogames: attempting to make the player's choice to play the game in the first place pose as a gesture of complicity. A contrived deus ex machina like this might work once, but even then it's a precious gimmick, one that hardly deserves the praise reserved for subtler methods.

Gaynor, Zimonja, and Nordhagen had worked together on a downloadable episode for *Bioshock 2* called "Minerva's Den." The campaign offers a deeper look into Rapture's operation via its central computing system. The promise and temptation of artificial intelligence takes the place of genetic modification, reiterating the series' overall one-bit moral klaxon by asserting that technologies are as good or bad as the men who use them.

Buoyed by success, Levine led the creation of another game in the series, *Bioshock Infinite,* which was released in 2013. *Infinite* promised a serious look at racism, religious fundamentalism, and American exceptionalism in another sci-fi secessionist dream-world, the floating city of Columbia. But *Infinite* betrayed its gorgeous and haunting opening sequence with a boring, mean-ingless onslaught of me-too first-person shooter carnage. On top of it, the game featured an inoculated female sidekick for the player's hunky alter ego. By now, critics had begun to grow impatient.[1]

So had Gaynor, Zimonja, and Nordhagen, who founded the Fullbright Company with the intention of opening the Pandora's box of narrative gaming that Levine wouldn't touch, having trad-ed curiosity for commercialism. Fullbright's design gambit: what would a game like *Bioshock* be like if you took out all the com-bat, all the violence, and just left the environment and the story? *Dear Esther,* released the year prior, had already taken a crack at the problem, but *Gone Home* aims for a less fragmentary, more traditional narrative experience, something normal people could relate to: a family's ordinary travails.

Many of *Bioshock*'s and *Dear Esther*'s approaches to environ-mental storytelling are retained in *Gone Home*: the exploration of space as a means for narrative progression, the use of recorded voice-overs activated by the discovery of specific items, a bleak moodiness that sets an overall tone, and a focus on environmental detail for world building.

Arbor House, the mansion that serves as *Gone Home*'s setting, is filled with various trinkets, most of which the player can pick up and investigate. The mid-1990s backdrop—a time before we conducted our lives entirely on computers and smartphones—offers an excuse for leaving material clues around. Some contain hidden clues or narrative threads that help explain the Greenbriar family's backstory: letters, postcards, files, cassettes. Others offer situational and temporal context: a *Pulp Fiction* ticket stub, VHS tapes, Magic Eye autostereograms. Others just offer texture, the lived-in details of an ordinary home: tissue boxes, books, foodstuffs.

Terry and Jan Greenbriar get coherent, discernible flaws and backstories, and their characters do change over the course of Katie's exploratory retelling. But Sam is really the star of *Gone Home*. Other than two stage-setting, one-line answering machine messages, hers is the voice we hear through the two to three hours that it takes to play *Gone Home,* as she recounts the events that led to her apparent disappearance.

This is a story of self-discovery by way of an adventure-game paean to riot grrrls. Outside Portland in the mid-1990s, Sam listens to Bratmobile and Heavens to Betsy with her girlfriend Lonnie. They dye their hair red, pass notes in school, and confide in each other in the big, empty spaces of Arbor House. Over time, they descend into slightly melodramatic but nonetheless charming teen love. As videogames lurch forward toward the questionable goal of narrative maturity, *Gone Home* would seem like a welcome, even an overdue, contribution to the cause. And it is.

But it's a brittle one. Everything fits together so well in *Gone Home* that the experience creaks and bends like the old house itself. Environmental storytelling is difficult because anything less than ontological fullness breaks the immersive promise of a lived-in world. And for the most part, Arbor House is empty, furnished to a minimum, the same sideboards and books, the same fixtures and accessories repeating from room to room. *Bioshock's* Rapture drew power mostly from its visual style, its intricate art deco design effectively suggesting that a drugged-out Objectivist civilization once lived within it. But the empty, ruined world has become too common in games, and *Gone Home* suffers for the sins of its predecessors.

There turn out to be credible reasons that the Greenbriar house is empty, but not enough reasons why the house is so barren. It sits uncomfortably between a theatrical stage on the one hand, and a realistic 3-D environment on the other. Onstage, any prop has a reason to be a gun that goes off in the second act, and a dearth of items never inspires incredulity. But a 3-D world requires a surfeit of extraneousness to make any single element's presence persuasive—not only an expensive feat, but also one that risks occluding the important papers, drawers, and cassette tapes among a sea of incidentals. At best, the result becomes a reasonably plausible setting for a semiplayable story. At worst, it amounts to a complicated menu system for selecting narrative fragments. Arbor House is most alive in its closets—an apt metaphor for the game's themes.

But more urgently, *Gone Home*'s characters are too archetypal to become truly literary. Katie suffers the least for this fault. She mostly functions as a cursor you move to experience the story, so gaps in her exposition are easily sorted out in the player's head. Perhaps because we are told so little about her, Katie is the most convincingly written character in *Gone Home*. A postcard from Paris found on a counter reveals Katie to be caring enough to remain connected, but also shows that she's largely going through the motions, doing what's expected—just the opposite of her sister: "I am in Paris," Katie writes. "I have done many Parisian things, including eating le petit dejeuner and wearing a beret." Writing is an art best cultivated with restraint.

Jan and Terry Greenbriar get short shrift in the game, which devotes the majority of its narrative attention and production effort to Sam. Absent voice acting, the game scatters the parents' backstories among fragments—letters, notes, post-its, and files. Jan's doubts about her marriage are assuaged by a letter from a friend, and Terry's troubled writing career is partly told through rejections from his publisher. As background noise, Jan and Terry are eminently credible, but as characters that make up half of the cast of *Gone Home,* the adults are mostly props, bit parts needed to advance Sam's storyline.

Eventually, the player discovers that Jan might have pondered a fling and that Terry's anxiety arises from a terrible secret. These revelations are significant, yet they are hidden in plain sight, a consequence of the game's commitment to connecting narrative progress with artifactual discovery. But more than that, they feel like pat choices, contrived plot devices that allow the game to appear sophisticated without taking any risks. Just as *Bioshock* referred to Objectivism without really engaging it, *Gone Home* evokes marital strife, professional anxiety, and childhood trauma for rhetorical rather than expressive reasons.

As for Sam, things are complicated. On the one hand, it's hard to justify criticizing a videogame for telling a teenage girl's queer coming-of-age story. But on the other hand, everything about that story is so neatly put into place, so clear and so paint-by-number, that it rings hollow. Not in its spirit, not in its message, even, but in its artistic achievement.

This is an unpopular opinion. *Gone Home* was met with almost universal praise in the gaming community, a world where numerical scores on a ten-point scale mean everything, and where *Gone Home* has achieved mostly nines and tens. After playing, dude-bro game dev celebrity Cliff Bleszinski gushed, "This game moved me in a way that I've never been moved by a game before." Lesbian, queer, and transgender players—an increasingly vocal and welcome counterpoint to traditional straight male voices in game development—penned love letters to the game, expressing how it captured their own teenage disquiet.[2]

It's impossible and undesirable to question these reactions, to undermine them with haughty disregard. But it's also not unreasonable to ask how these players could have been so easily satisfied. For readers of contemporary fiction or even viewers of serious television, it's hard for me to imagine that *Gone Home* would elicit much of any reaction, let alone the reports of full-bore weeping and breathless panegyrics this game has enjoyed. I felt charmed upon completing *Gone Home,* but then I felt ashamed for failing to meet the emotional bar set by my videogame-playing brethren.

Compared with classic and contemporary works of literature on the challenges and implications of queer love (Virginia Woolf's *Orlando,* or Lillian Hellman's *Children's Hour,* or Pamela Moore's

Chocolates for Breakfast, or Alice Walker's *Color Purple,* or Bertha
Harris's *Lover,* or Rita Mae Brown's *Rubyfruit Jungle,* to name but
a few of the most obvious candidates), *Gone Home* would seem
amateurish, forced, heavy-handed. Even Gary D. Wilson's "Sweet
Sixteen," a five-hundred-word microfiction about teenage love
and its midlife aftermath, makes *Gone Home* feel trite and boiler-
plate.[3] For a literary audience, *Gone Home* will certainly be more
appealing than *Bioshock*—but less appealing than, say, Jeanette
Winterson's *Oranges Are Not the Only Fruit,* a book *Bioshock*
players have no more heard of than readers of Winterson have
heard of Ken Levine.

Maybe we are not meant to weigh *Gone Home* against time-
tested works of narrative accomplishment. But if not, then by
what measure shall we judge it? *Gone Home* gets the praise one
would associate with Alfonso Cuarón-does-*7th Guest* or Sarah
Waters-does-*Myst,* when in reality it's more like John Hughes-
does-*7th Guest* or Judy Blume-does-*Myst.* It's a literary work on
the level of young adult fiction.

And you know, that's not bad! Hughes's movies and Blume's
books have a place in the world, and that place is not necessarily
better or worse than Jim Jarmusch films or Roberto Bolaño novels.
But it is *different,* and that difference makes a difference.

There is an idea among the game-playing and development
communities that games can be stories with interactivity and that
such new types of stories are going to "broaden the audience" for
games. But this is a flawed idea, because a broadened audience
would mean an audience amenable to such new material in the
context of their existing tastes. If that gap is not acknowledged
and addressed, then we end up with games as *bad* television
shows and novels—bad television shows and novels with button
pressing.

Then again, what if *Gone Home* teaches us that videogames
need only grow up enough to meet the expectations other narrative media have reset in the meantime? After all, we're living in
an age in which the literary mainstream is dominated by young

adult fiction anyway. Adults read series like *Harry Potter* and *Twilight* and *The Hunger Games* with unabashed glee. Comic book film adaptations have overtaken the cinema. What if games haven't failed to mature so much as all other media have degenerated, such that the model of the young adult novel is really the highest (and most commercially viable) success one can achieve in narrative?

As the designer Merritt Kopas said of *Gone Home*, "This is a videogame. About girls in love. That shouldn't be exceptional in and of itself, but it is."[4] And there's the rub. Because Kopas is right: the fact of the game's very existence becomes more important than its aesthetic ambitions. Such is the remaining not-so-hidden secret of *Gone Home*, a game about not-so-hidden secrets: that media must struggle against increasingly strong rhetorical currents to have even a chance at spawning a modicum of expression before dying off.

If *Gone Home* is meant to introduce the gamer community to a representational possibility space that includes girls in love, listless wives, and dispirited writers, then we must fess up to an inconvenient truth: that even a game that looks beyond one kind of adolescence still does so through the lens of another. A game set among the riot grrrl 1990s shames games for how late they are to the party: third-wave feminism is over twenty years old, born just after videogames had abandoned their first, now-forgotten drive toward the cultural mainstream via political simulations and adventure games to settle on a steady diet of obliterating hell-spawn and saving kidnapped princesses. Perhaps the coming-of-age story told in *Gone Home* is not just Sam's but that of videogames themselves. The *very idea* that the very idea of a game about a lesbian girl could surprise us should also embarrass us.

Adolescence is videogame culture's greatest fear. That we will forever be stuck with juvenile power fantasies: fast cars, Big Fucking Guns, and boob physics. That videogames will be lost to adulthood like comic books once were. Just as Katie Greenbriar comes home to a home that isn't a home for anyone, so *Gone*

Home reveals a secret that turns out to be an obvious one, and one much bigger than videogames: today, narrative *writ large* is mired in a permanent adolescence that videogames can now easily equal, the modest, subtle pleasures of the literary arts melting under Iron Man's turbines, impaled by Katniss Everdeen's arrow.

Eventually adolescence ends, and we leave it. Unless it has fixed itself as our greatest aspiration. After all, comic books aren't a ghetto, at all; they are bigger and more mainstream than ever. What if escaping one kind of adolescence entails embracing a different one, from the other direction? The promise of *Gone Home* is also its hazard: not just that it offers a well-needed alternative to videogames' immaturity, but also that it offers *enough* of one to satisfy us. That pubescence's salve is more pubescence, but inverted. That coming-of-age has arrived, and that its arrival is sufficient.

CONCLUSION

Anything but Games

Not doing game criticism

When I started doing game criticism, even using the phrase *game criticism* felt like a word-of-faith name-it-and-claim-it affair. The idea that there could be game criticism, that one could exert the critical muscle on games—it seemed unlikely and even preposterous. It was its own outcome, the curiosity that replaced example. I saw myself trying out some methods and examples of that process rather than trying to found a field or a discipline or a method, or to become known as a game critic. If the latter things happened—and I'm not sure they did—then they happened by accident.

And maybe not just as fluke but also as mishap. The world of videogames is still imbued with indignity, plagued by its own tendency to self-humiliation.

Some time ago, I was talking to a friend in technology media. "Sometimes I wonder why I'm in tech," he started saying. He paused for a beat. "Then I think, at least I'm not in games."

Why would he feel this way? Because of games' provincialism.

I don't just mean the old-hat, stereotypical image of gamers as teenage boys in basements engorging Doritos and knocking back Mountain Dew, although clearly that image is still very much in circulation. Rather, I mean that games have often maintained a separation from other forms of human culture and creativity. And that they—that we—have actively cultured and supported this separation in order to come into our own.

Even as games have become ever more widespread they have also receded farther within themselves. And among the

< 181 >

communities that would bother reading a relatively esoteric book like the one you hold in your hands right now (game scholars; avid players; indie developers; the stray, curious everyman), it's easy to pat ourselves on the back and say, "but it's different for us." And it is.

But also, it isn't.

Just think about the ways we distribute and sell games—especially the indie games like *Proteus* and *Gone Home* and *Surgeon Simulator* that are supposedly enacting a deliberate expressive revolution to counter the unvoiced anonymity of *Bully* and *Medal of Honor* and their ilk.

The digital distribution service Steam has made independence financially viable at times, but it has done so by recapitulating the aesthetic of the videogame retail experience—the dark, weird, embarrassing game shop re-created as a tiny-text, black-and-gunmetal interface through which all further activity is sieved. In this brave new world, one is discouraged even to run games away from Valve's supervision. Better to access them from the Steam Client, where play time can be tracked for later boasting on its internal community network. Encountering games still requires pledging fealty to gamedom.

Entering a games retail outlet is a lot like entering a sex shop or a liquor store. The game shop deals solely in the equipment of a different kind of sin, the sin of empty diversion—at least in the eyes of those who turn their noses up at the practice. But even among those who embrace rather than recoil at games, game shops are still vaguely unseemly. Slightly grimy and unbecoming, where one surreptitiously plunks down cash in advance for the latest dark, brooding, big-dude shooter or trades in the spent disc of the last one.

By contrast, neither sex nor liquor takes on quite the same tenor outside the specialty shop as it does within one. In the bar or the club, for example, conversation and dance cut the strength of booze, even if drink remains the lubricant for these other social practices. There's something about a whole retail establishment devoted to a singular practice of any kind that just sits strange. It implies perversion, excess.

Buying games wasn't always such a specialized affair. I first encountered the 1986 Macintosh title *Dark Castle* in a special alcove of the shopping mall book retailer B. Dalton. Videogames in a bookstore are different from video games in a videogame store. In a bookstore—even a mall store of questionable cultural virtue—they become one kind of media alongside others, intermixed with novels and self-help, cookbooks and cartoons. The bookstore cuts the lewdness of games just as the pub cuts the decadence of drinking.

That alcove in B. Dalton would be spun off as Software Etc. in 1987. A little more than a decade later, after a series of bankruptcies, mergers, and sales, the chain would re-emerge as GameStop. In 2014 the retailer brought in over $9 billion in global revenue. Today, games are found mostly in specialty shops like these, or secured behind glass cases or in plastic lockboxes within big box retailers like Best Buy and Target and Walmart. There, they become consumer electronics accessories akin to headphones rather than cultural media artifacts akin to books.

When games moved to the Internet, at first they did so under the anonymity of all online commerce: as commodities suspended in the generic blankness of a retail webpage. The web actually returned games to the menagerie of other media—like a book or a film or a record, a game was just another product that would arrive in a parcel at your door two days hence, or that would load in a browser like a video or an animation.

But soon, online game retail bifurcated into two different worlds, each of which doubled down on a different bet.

On one side: Facebook app directories and the Apple App Store and their ilk. These methods signaled a return to the mall bookshop approach, albeit in a different way. Games became baubles and gewgaws, pleasant little media creatures sold alongside ebooks and music singles or delivered between profile pictures and status updates. They became integrated into the vernacular of online and smartphone life.

On the other side: the digital version of the specialty retailers. Steam and the PSN and Xbox Live console stores. As at the sex shop, a special, committed knowledge is required even to make sense of these services. They involve special, dedicated hardware and software installations, intricate, custom-created interface grammars, and idiosyncratic interaction models. Even commerce is unseemly here, where the shroud of redemption codes and pre-paid cards make ordinary transactions seem sordid.

These services repeat the unlearned history of Software Etc. and GameStop before them. By fencing off games into exclusive outlets, they make the very idea of a game subject to the special practices and identities of those who would commit to becoming the devoted patrons of such outlets. This sequestration is clearest on Steam, where even the act of playing a game is siphoned through a specialized client that tracks play time and lures you into peripheral activities like message boards and trading cards. Even unusual indie games of potentially general interest demand that their audiences tolerate the inhospitable griminess of this foreign service in order to buy them.

In the digital retail ecosystem, the app stores have become associated with schlock and kitsch among purportedly serious gamers. But the tawdry main street helps counteract the bawdy underworld. When games feel like a product one can buy out in the open, they become more normalized, more ordinary, more proper. In that respect, games' overall repute might correspond with how little shame people feel when buying them.

All of that—that's an example of what I mean by games' provincialism.

The downside of having arrived—of having games books and games degrees and games festivals and games retail channels and games communities—is thinking that their influence and their impact extend farther than they really do.

Yes, diverse games are here to an extent. There are games

about being a teenage lesbian and games about the alienation of otherness and games about being an inanimate geologic formation, even. Lots of people are making games, and some of those games are often reaching substantial audiences. But, like it or not, games are still a niche tricked by the echo chamber of internal success into thinking that they are approaching the mainstream.

The truth is, the general public downloads whatever they heard about from a friend on the App Store or whatever appears at the top of the charts. The truth is, games have so long wavered between affinity with Silicon Valley and jealousy of Hollywood that they have effectively found home in neither. The truth is, *Minecraft* is a game for children. The truth is, when I write at a "smart general readership" magazine like *The Atlantic,* an order of magnitude more people read me when I write about the McRib or Google or even *Star Trek* than when I write about videogames.[1] The truth is, a book like this one is doomed to relatively modest sales and an even more modest readership, despite the generous support of the university press that publishes it and despite the fact that I am fortunate enough to have a greater reach than the average game critic. Elsewhere, my extended colleagues have set out to create their own small presses for games writing because you can't sell a trade book on games like you can sell one on social media or even on *Star Wars,* because games are considered to have no audience.[2]

Admittedly, this isn't necessarily a problem. There's no reason any art form needs to be mainstream, and indeed it's easy to argue why one shouldn't be. But it's perilous for games' sense of cultural place to be at odds with their reality.

And actually, this isn't a phenomenon limited to games. In the *Washington Post,* Alyssa Rosenberg writes about what she calls the "new culture war." "As the new culture war has widened," Rosenberg says, "it has also fragmented, turning less into a clash of great powers than into a series of intractable guerrilla conflicts, marked by shifting alliances and the rapid emergence of new players."[3]

Whereas previously culture fought, won, and lost its battles at the scale of mass media—think of Madonna and Bart Simpson and Murphy Brown—now we do so in isolated pockets of niche media hobbyism. Rosenberg sees this as an unexpected victory. "Everyone can win the new culture wars," she declares, because "all stories have a chance to be told."

The problem with Rosenberg's account is that fragmentation becomes Balkanization, which becomes recuperated into Libertarianism. Mutual hostility becomes "do what you want, just don't foist it on me." Pushed to its limits, all fandom becomes apartheid.

Games have come of age—*again,* I might add, as they do every decade or so, to fanfare already forgotten—in the age of Rosenberg's new culture wars. So not only are we fighting civil wars among ourselves, we are doing so in a tiny, peripheral, war-torn medium already written off by the "developed" media ecosystem. From outside, people have the same prognosis for videogames that they have about, say, Somalia.

This state of affairs ought to chasten us. It ought to revise our understanding of the scope of the work before us.

There's another kind of diversity beyond the diversity of representation among players, creators, and characters. There's also the diversity of our interests and our dispositions, of the company we keep and the influences that inspire us, the people and the groups and the industries and the materials that we contact. It has to do with having dealings enough with the world such that it is no longer possible to be seen as a parochial backwater not even worth opposing let alone supporting.

We have become too comfortable here in games. We have our own dialects now, our own customs via Steam and Twitch and Let's Plays and festivals and so on. Dialects and customs are useful because they allow us to dispense with constant explanation. They are what allow me to reference games in the pages above and assume that you, the reader, will be sufficiently familiar with them to process my arguments about them. Or else, that you'll know where to learn more and that you'll have sufficient motivation to do so.

Before these customs and resources existed, things were worse when they were more nascent, but they were better because it was impossible to run only in the circles of games. We were all here from somewhere else—from painting, from architecture, from advertising, from computing, from systems theory, from toy design, from literature. That's where I came from, from elsewhere. Sometimes we saw those connections as baggage or even as colonialism, but they also offered grounding. They helped root games amid broader contexts. They connected us to bedrock.

But here's the thing about broader contexts: new ones might not be possible anymore. We can't reject them, we can't "disrupt" them or ignore them because we have staked out our own little island amid rising oceans. Games can survive on their own, but perhaps only in the same way that Somalia can—as a world unto itself. There are no games as the dominant medium of the twenty-first century, because there is no dominant medium of the twenty-first century. There's only shrapnel.

We need to stop fighting against this fact as if it were a war we could win, that anybody could. We've shoved off from shipwreck desert islands on makeshift rafts to make landfall—on other desert islands. And we can make civilization here. Just look around, on your bookshelf, among your Twitter followers, amid your Twitch viewers, on your PSN or Steam friends list, at PAX or Dragon Con or IndieCade. These are communities that each of us could choose to make our only community. The question is, will it be enough? Do we care if people can still get away with saying "at least I'm not in games" and for it to be a *reasonable statement* that produces knowing nods?

The era of fields and disciplines had ended. The era of critical communities had ended. And the very idea of game criticism risks Balkanizing games writing from other writing, severing it from the rivers and fields that would sustain it. Game criticism is subsistence criticism. There's not enough land to till in games alone. Nor in literature alone, nor in toasters alone. God save us from a future of game critics, gnawing on scraps like the zombies that fester in our objects of study.

We can be game players without being *just* game players. And amid today's fragmented media ecosystem, it's even more urgent that we send more envoys outside our circles. Otherwise, it will seem no less perverse to be a maker or a critic of games than it already does to be a player of them. Instead we must desire something simpler and less dramatic: for games to be here among us, like the fine arts, like media, but also like fashion, like carpeting, like toasters. And most often, like all of these things and more, all at once, their many facets glinting in the many lights of influence and context in which they bathe. Eventually, we might hope, books like this won't be necessary or even possible, because games will no longer make sense as a domain unto themselves, an elsewhere we go for stimulation or for worship. Instead, they will prevail by being a thing among others, ebbing and flowing into and out of our attention and commitment, taking their place as one among an infinity of dreams and inspirations, diversions and obsessions. No less like toasters on countertops than like serigraphs under glass, like thick, green summer lawns, like overstuffed burritos, like emotionally manipulative, Oscar-chasing dramatic films. What kind of madness or zealotry would it entail to obsess over one of these subjects alone? And yet, magically, by distributing that same madness across all those targets and more, we achieve a new sanity. And we nickname that new sanity "the world," and it's where we live, and dream, and watch, and toast, and play.

Notes

Introduction

1. Barry Schwartz, *The Paradox of Choice: Why Less Is More* (New York: Ecco, 2003), 1–12.

2. Jason Schreier, "Why Are Game Developer Bonuses Based on Review Scores?," *Kotaku,* March 15, 2012, http://kotaku.com/5893595 /why-are-game-developer-bonuses-based-on-review-scores.

3. Respectively, http://www.amazon.com/Images-SI-Uranium -Ore/dp/B000796XXM and http://www.amazon.com/Tuscan-Whole -Milk-Gallon-128/dp/B00032G1SO/.

1. The Squalid Grace of *Flappy Bird*

1. Sarah Perez, "Developer behind '*Flappy Bird,*' the Impossible Game Blowing Up the App Store, Says He Just Got Lucky," *TechCrunch,* February 1, 2014, http://techcrunch.com/2014/02/01/developer -behind-flappy-bird-the-impossible-game-blowing-up-the-app-store -says-he-just-got-lucky/.

2. Elaine Heney, "How to Make *Flappy Bird,* #1 App—Interview with Game Developer Dong Nguyen: Updated," *Chocolate App Labs,* January 31, 2014, http://www.thechocolatelabapps.com/how -to-make-flappy-bird/.

3. Aaron Richardson, "I Hate *Flappy Bird,* but I Can't Stop Playing It," *n3rdabl3,* January 31, 2014, http://www.n3rdabl3.co.uk/.

4. Dean Takahashi, "Nine Reasons Why *Flappy Bird* Has Become the Latest Viral Gaming Hit," *VentureBeat,* February 1, 2014, http:// venturebeat.com/2014/02/01/9-reasons-why-flappy-bird-has-become -the-latest-viral-gaming-hit/.

5. Simon Parkin, "Don't Stop: The Game That Conquered Smartphones," *New Yorker,* June 7, 2013, http://www.newyorker.com

< 189 >

/online/blogs/elements/2013/06/the-revival-of-a-long-lost-gaming
-genre.html.

2. A Portrait of the Artist as a Game Studio

1. John Geirland, "Go with the Flow," *Wired*, September, 1996, http://www.wired.com/wired/archive/4.09/czik_pr.html.

2. Jenova Chen, "Flow in Games" (master's thesis, University of Southern California, 2006), http://www.jenovachen.com/flowin games/thesis.htm.

4. Little Black Sambo, I'm Going to Eat You Up!

1. Zachary Reese, "And Yet 'Wasp' Produces Some Sort of Insect," *Stress Lines* (blog), September 16, 2009, http://stresslines.org/?p=598.

2. Helen Bannerman, *The Story of Little Black Sambo* (London: Grant Richards, 1899).

3. William Black, "How Watermelons Became a Racist Trope," *The Atlantic*, December 8, 2014, http://www.theatlantic.com/national /archive/2014/12/how-watermelons-became-a-racist-trope/383529/.

4. Brian Ashcraft, "Racial Term in DS' Scribblenauts? Unintentional, Developer Explains," *Kotaku*, September 16, 2009, http://kotaku.com/5361276/racial-term-in-ds-scribblenauts -unintended-developer-explains-update?skyline=true&s=x.

5. Calamity, "Because We Can't Have Nice Things: *Scribblenauts* Racism! Breaking!," *NeoGaf*, September 17, 2009, http://www.neogaf .com/forum/showthread.php?t=374412; J. C. Fletcher, "5th Cell: *Scribblenauts*' Scandalous-Looking 'Sambo' Item Is a Misunderstand- ing," *Joystiq*, September 16, 2009, http://www.joystiq.com/2009 /09/16/5th-cell-scribblenauts-scandalous-looking-sambo-item-is -a-mi/.

6. Fletcher, "5th Cell."

7. Night_Trekker, comment on Calamity, "Because We Can't."

8. TRT-X, comment on Ashcraft, "Racial Term."

9. ShadowOdin is gonna be King of Kotaku, comment on Ashcraft, "Racial Term."

10. Leslie Katz, "Koran Expressions Delay PS3 Title 'Little Big Planet,'" *CNET*, October 20, 2008, http://www.cnet.com/news /koran-expressions-delay-ps3-title-little-big-planet/.

11. Jim Sterling, "Should We Boycott *Shadow Complex?*," *Destructoid*, August 23, 2009, http://www.destructoid.com/should -we-boycott-shadow-complex--145354.phtml.

12. Barack Obama, "Race" (speech, Philadelphia, March 18, 2008), *CNN*, http://www.cnn.com/2008/POLITICS/03/18/obama.transcript/.

5. Can a Gobbler Have It All?

1. Preston Burt, "The Crazy and Profitable Origin of *Ms. Pac-Man*," *Arcade Sushi*, December 27, 2013, http://arcadesushi.com /the-crazy-and-profitable-origin-of-ms-pac-man/.

2. Steve Golson, "From *Crazy Otto* to *Ms. Pac-Man*," *California Extreme 2012*, July 28, 2012.

3. The removal of the hair apparently came from Namco president Masaya Nakamura (Burt, "Crazy and Profitable Origin of *Ms. Pac-Man*").

4. Joyce Worley, "Women Join the Arcade Revolution," *Electronic Games Monthly*, May 1982, 31–32.

5. Steven L. Kent, *The Ultimate History of Video Games* (New York: Three Rivers Press, 2001), 171–72.

6. Eve Kay, "Call Me Ms.," *Guardian*, June 28, 2007, http://www .theguardian.com/world/2007/jun/29/gender.uk.

7. Ibid.

6. Racketeer Sports

1. Craig A. Anderson and Karen E. Dill, "Video Games and Aggressive Thoughts, Feelings, and Behavior in the Laboratory and in Life," *Journal of Personality and Social Psychology* 78, no. 4 (2000): 772.

2. Amy Graff, "Do Violent Video Games Lead Kids to Be Violent in the Real World?," *SFGate*, February 22, 2013, http://blog.sfgate.com /sfmoms/2013/02/22/do-violent-video-games-lead-kids-to-be -violent-in-the-real-world.

3. "NRA Calls Out Violence in Video Games, Cites 'Kindergarten Killers,'" *FoxNews.com*, December 21, 2012, http://www.foxnews.com /tech/2012/12/21/nra-calls-out-violence-in-video-games-like -kindergarten-killers/.

4. Anderson and Dill, "Video Games and Aggressive Thoughts," 772–90.

5. Geoffrey R. Loftus and Elizabeth F. Loftus, *Mind at Play: The Psychology of Video Games* (New York: Basic Books, 1983).

6. Loftus and Loftus, *Mind at Play*, 100.

7. "Mark Pincus Talk at Startup@Berkeley," *Vimeo* video, 34:25, posted by "Startup Berkeley," March 18, 2009, http://vimeo.com /3738428.

8. Megan Rose Dickey, "Insanely Popular Game *Candy Crush Saga* Is Bringing In an Estimated $633,000 a Day," *Business Insider*, July 8, 2013, http://www.businessinsider.com/candy-crush-saga -daily-revenue-2013-7.

9. Based on Think Gaming Inc. revenue estimates. *Candy Crush Saga*'s can be found here: http://thinkgaming.com/app-sales-data/2 /candy-crush-saga/. As of January 14, 2015, Think Gaming estimated the game's daily take at $931,287; by July of that year, $954,372.

10. Stuart Dredge, "*Candy Crush Saga*: '70% of the People on the Last Level Haven't Paid Anything,'" *Guardian*, September 10, 2013, http://www.theguardian.com/technology/appsblog/2013/sep/10 /candy-crush-saga-king-interview.

11. Earl L. Grinols, "Economics of Gambling," *U.S. Economic Directions*, April 24, 2012, http://blogs.baylor.edu/earl_grinols/about /gambling-economics/.

12. Matt Lynley, "The Biggest Losers from Zynga's Stock Crash," *Business Insider*, August 3, 2012, http://www.businessinsider.com /the-biggest-losers-of-zyngas-stock-crash-2012-8?op=1.

8. Can the Other Come Out and Play?

1. Raph Koster, "Are Single-Player Games Doomed?," *Raph Koster's Website*, February 10, 2006, http://www.raphkoster.com/2006/02/10 /are-single-player-games-doomed/.

2. See, in particular, Johan Huizinga, *Homo Ludens: A Study of the Play Element in Culture* (London: Routledge, 1949); and Brian Sutton-Smith, *The Ambiguity of Play* (Cambridge, Mass.: Harvard University Press, 2001).

9. A Way of Looking

1. Jay David Bolter and Diane Gromala, *Windows and Mirrors: Interaction Design, Digital Art, and the Myth of Transparency* (Cambridge, Mass.: MIT Press, 2003), 34, 74.

2. Nate Ahearn, "A Bold Leap That Doesn't Nail the Landing," *IGN*, November 11, 2008, http://www.ign.com/articles/2008/11/11 /mirrors-edge-review.

3. Keith Stuart, "Do Game Reviewers Really Understand Innovation?," *Guardian*, November 14, 2008, http://www.guardian .co.uk/technology/gamesblog/2008/nov/14/gameculture-playstation1.

4. Leigh Alexander, "Scattershot on My Way Out," *Sexy Videogameland* (blog), November 26, 2008, https://web.archive .org/web/20090317185918/http://sexyvideogameland.blogspot .com/2008/11/scattershot-on-my-way-out.html.

5. Leigh Alexander, "Stop Making Sense," *Sexy Videogameland* (blog), December 10, 2008, https://web.archive.org/web/20110109 035824/http://sexyvideogameland.blogspot.com/2008/12/stop -making-sense.html.

10. Free Speech Is Not a Marketing Plan

1. "*Medal of Honor,*" Electronic Arts, accessed November 25, 2014, http://www.ea.com/medal-of-honor.

2. Michael Ciply and Brooks Barnes, "Disney Sells Miramax for $660 Million," *New York Times*, July 30, 2010, http://www .nytimes.com/2010/07/31/business/media/31miramax.html; Michael Arrington, "Playdom Acquired by Disney for Up to $763.2 Million," *TechCrunch*, July 27, 2010, http://techcrunch.com/2010/07/27 /playdom-acquired-by-disney-for-up-to-763-2-million.

3. Nick Cowen, "Liam Fox calls for Medal Of Honor to Be Banned," *Telegraph*, August 23, 2010, http://www.telegraph.co.uk/technology /video-games/7960031/Liam-Fox-calls-for-Medal-Of-Honor-to-be -banned.html.

4. "Video Game Lets You Be the Taliban," *Fox News* video, 4:17, August 14, 2010, http://video.foxnews.com/v/4311300/video -game-lets-you-be-the-taliban/.

5. Brian Crecente, "Video Game Pulled Globally from Military Stores over Taliban Inclusion," *Kotaku*, September 9, 2010, http:// kotaku.com/5628741/gamestop-pulls-video-game-from-military -stores-over-taliban-inclusion.

6. Brian Crecente, "Electronic Arts Buckles under Pressure, Removes Playable Taliban from *Medal of Honor,*" *Kotaku*, October 1, 2010, http://kotaku.com/5653024/

electronic-arts-buckles-under-pressure-removes-taliban-from-medal
-of-honor.

7. Brian Crecente, "Playable Taliban Jeopardized U.S. Army's
Support for *Medal of Honor*," *Kotaku*, October 1, 2010, http://kotaku
.com/5653601/playable-taliban-jeopardized-us-armys-support-for
-medal-of-honor.

8. Chris Remo, "The Meaning of *Medal of Honor*," *Gamasutra*,
October 1, 2010, http://www.gamasutra.com/view/feature/6156/the
_meaning_of_medal_of_honor.php.

11. Shaking the Holocaust Train

1. Adam Hartley, "Hands on: Nintendo's Wii MotionPlus,"
TechRadar, March 24, 2009, http://www.techradar.com/us/news
/gaming/hands-on-nintendo-s-wii-motionplus-587634.

2. EWAdams [Ernest Adams], May 1, 2009 (7:04 a.m.), comment
on Jordan Deam, "TGC 2009: How a Board Game Can Make You Cry,"
The Escapist Forums, The Escapist, April 30, 2009, http://www
.escapistmagazine.com/forums/read/6.110665-TGC-2009-How-a
-Board-Game-Can-Make-You-Cry.

12. The Long Shot

1. "Francis Ford-Coppola Interview: Filmmaker, Producer, and
Screenwriter," *Academy of Achievement*, June 17, 1994, http://www
.achievement.org/autodoc/page/cop0int-1.

13. Puzzling the Sublime

1. Gilles Deleuze and Félix Guattari, *A Thousand Plateaus*, trans.
Brian Massumi (Minneapolis: University of Minnesota Press, 1987), 352.

2. *Wikipedia*, s.v. "Water, Gas, and Electricity," last modified
September 3, 2014, https://en.wikipedia.org/wiki/Water,_gas,_and
_electricity.

3. Janet Murray, *Hamlet on the Holodeck* (New York: Free Press,
1997), 144.

4. Markku Eskelinen, "The Gaming Situation," *Game Studies* 1,
no. 1 (2001), http://gamestudies.org/0101/eskelinen.

5. Immanuel Kant, *Critique of Judgment*, trans. J. H. Bernard (New
York: Hafner, 1951), 86–89.

6. Ibid.

16. What Is a Sports Videogame?

1. Fares Kayali and Peter Purgathofer, "Two Halves of Play-Simulation versus Abstraction and Transformation in Sports Videogames Design," *Eludamos: Journal for Computer Game Culture* 2, no. 1 (2008): 105–27. So uninterested are many critics and scholars in sports games that the popularity of this sentiment becomes difficult to substantiate. It's a claim more often made at the bar or coffee shop than in books and journals. One example—although it's hardly as derogatory in tone as some game critics might like—can be found in Kayali and Purgathofer, "Two Halves of Play-Simulation."

2. Ernest Adams and Andrew Rollings, *Fundamentals of Game Design* (New York: New Riders, 2006), 482.

3. Jan Harold Brunvand, *The Study of American Folklore: An Introduction,* 3rd ed. (New York: Norton, 1986), 378–81; Brunvand, ed., *American Folklore: An Encyclopedia* (New York: Routledge, 2006), 660–61.

4. Ludwig Wittgenstein, *Philosophical Investigations,* trans. G. E. M. Anscombe, P. M. S. Hacker, and Joachim Schulte (New York: Wiley, 1953), sec. 66.

5. Jacques Derrida, *Limited Inc.,* trans. Samuel Weber (Evanston, Ill.: Northwestern University Press, 1988), 62.

6. George Eden Marindin, "The Game of 'Harpastum' or 'Pheninda,'" *Classical Review* 4, no. 4 (1890): 145–49.

7. Ibid., 146.

8. Ibid.

9. Ibid., 148.

10. Ibid., 148–49.

11. Abe Stein, Mia Consalvo, and Konstantin Mitgutsch, "Who Are Sports Gamers? A Large Scale Study of Sports Video Game Players," *Convergence: The International Journal of Research into New Media Technologies* (2012), doi:10.1177/1354856512459840.

12. John Constantine, "The Indoor Kid's Guide to *Madden,*" 1up.com, August 28, 2009, https://web.archive.org/web/20130306015254 /http://www.1up.com/features/hardcore-gamers-madden-players.

13. T. L. Taylor, *Raising the Stakes: E-Sports and the Professionalization of Computer Gaming* (Cambridge, Mass.: MIT Press, 2012), chap. 5.

17. The Agony of Mastery

1. Helen Philips, "Paranormal Beliefs Linked to Brain Chemistry," *New Scientist,* July 27, 2002, http://www.newscientist.com/article /dn2589-paranormal-beliefs-linked-to-brain-chemistry.html.

2. James Hookway, "'*Flappy Bird*' Creator Pulled Game Because It Was 'Too Addictive,'" *Wall Street Journal,* last updated February 11, 2014, http://online.wsj.com/news/articles/SB10001424052702303874 504579376323271110900.

3. "Fish Plays *Pokémon,*" Twitch video, accessed November 30, 2014, http://www.twitch.tv/fishplayspokemon.

18. The Abyss between the Human and the Alpine

1. "Films," David O'Reilly's website, accessed November 30, 2014, www.davidO'Reilly.com/films/.

2. David O'Reilly, "Basic Animation Aesthetics," David O'Reilly's website, accessed November 30, 2014, http://files.davidO'Reilly.com /downloads/BasicAnimationAesthetics.pdf.

3. Andrew Webster, "Playing a Mountain Simulation Is Surprisingly Emotional: The Creator of a Fake Game from *Her* Returns with a Real One Called *Mountain,*" *The Verge,* July 1, 2014, http://www .theverge.com/2014/7/1/5857458/mountain-game.

4. Ibid.

5. Brendan Keogh, "Thoughts on Why I Am Unable to Appreciate *Mountain,*" *Ungaming,* July 9, 2014, http://ungaming.tumblr.com/.

19. Word Games Last Forever

1. Larry Frum, "Five Years on, Millions Still Dig 'FarmVille,'" *CNN,* July 31, 2014, http://www.cnn.com/2014/07/31/tech/gaming-gadgets /farmville-fifth-anniversary.

2. Leigh Alexander, "Zach Gage Tackles a Genre He Hates with *SpellTower,*" *Gamasutra,* November 17, 2011, http://www.gamasutra .com/view/news/128208/Zach_Gage_Tackles_A_Genre_He_Hates _With_SpellTower.php.

20. Perpetual Adolescence

1. Daniel Golding, "*BioShock Infinite*: An Intelligent, Violent Videogame?," *ABC Arts* (blog), *Australian Broadcasting Corporation,*

April 9, 2013, http://www.abc.net.au/arts/stories/s3733057.htm; and Leigh Alexander, "Now Is the Best Time: A Critique of *BioShock Infinite*," *Kotaku*, April 11, 2013, http://kotaku.com/now-is-the-best -time-a-critique-of-bioshock-infinite-472517493.

2. Laura Kate, "Just Take Me Seriously—A Personal Slice of *Gone Home*," *Indie Haven*, August 22, 2013, http://indiehaven.com /just-take-me-seriously-a-personal-slice-of-gone-home.

3. Gary D. Wilson, "Sweet Sixteen," in *Flash Fiction Forward: Eighty Very Short Stories*, ed. Robert Shapard and James Thomas (New York: W. W. Norton, 2006), 26–27.

4. Merritt Kopas, "On *Gone Home*," *Merritt Kopas* (blog), August 17, 2013, mkopas.net/2013/08/on-gone-home/.

Conclusion

1. Respectively: Ian Bogost, "McRib: Enjoy Your Symptom," *The Atlantic*, November 13, 2013, http://www.theatlantic.com/technology /archive/2013/11/the-mcrib-enjoy-your-symptom/281413/; Bogost, "What Is 'Evil' to Google?," *The Atlantic*, October 15, 2013, http://www .theatlantic.com/technology/archive/2013/10/what-is-evil-to-google /280573/; Bogost, "Shaka, When the Walls Fell," *The Atlantic*, June 18, 2014, http://www.theatlantic.com/entertainment/archive/2014/06 /star-treking-tng-and-the-limits-of-language-shaka-when-the-walls -fell/372107/.

2. "About Us," Boss Fight Books, accessed November 30, 2014, http://bossfightbooks.com/pages/about.

3. Alyssa Rosenberg, "The Culture Wars Are Back, and This Time, Everyone Can Win," *Washington Post*, October 8, 2014, http:// www.washingtonpost.com/news/act-four/wp/2014/10/08/the-culture -wars-are-back-and-this-time-everyone-can-win/.

Electronic Mediations

Series Editors: N. Katherine Hayles, Peter Krapp, Rita Raley, and Samuel Weber
Founding Editor: Mark Poster

IAN BOGOST is Ivan Allen College Distinguished Chair in Media Studies and professor of interactive computing at the Georgia Institute of Technology, where he also holds an appointment in the Scheller College of Business. He is founding partner at Persuasive Games LLC, an independent game studio, and a contributing editor at *The Atlantic*. He is author of many books, including *How to Do Things with Videogames* (Minnesota, 2011) and *Alien Phenomenology, or What It's Like to Be a Thing* (Minnesota, 2012).